Good News for the Fainthearted

Good News for the Fainthearted

A Devotional Workbook for Mothers of Young Children

Lauren Davis

Copyright © 2021 Lauren Davis
ISBN: 9798733488660
All rights reserved.
No part of this publication may be reproduced
without permission in writing from the author.
Unless otherwise indicated,
all Scripture quotations are from The Holy Bible,
English Standard Version® (ESV®), copyright © 2001 by Crossway,
a publishing ministry of Good News Publishers.
Used by permission. All rights reserved.

*"For Zion's sake I will not keep silent,
and for Jerusalem's sake I will not be quiet."*
Isaiah 62:1

This workbook belongs to: _____

Good News for the Fainthearted

A Devotional Workbook
for Mothers of Young Children

Contents

Introduction		iii
How to Use This Book		v
An Introductory Prayer		vii
1	Say "Yes"	1
2	He Takes Me by the Hand	5
3	For the Glory of His Name	10
4	Love of Christ	15
5	Follow	20
6	Be Strong	25
7	Glad and Confident	30
8	Awake, O Sleeper	35
9	Praise	39
10	It Is a Good Day	43
Reflection		47
11	Abundance	49
12	Blessed Work	54
13	Burdened	59
14	He Will Establish Your Plans	64
15	Attention	69
16	Our Cause	74
17	Think About These Things	79
18	Dig Deep	84
19	The Lord Disciplines	88
20	Pain	93

Reflection   99

21	BOW	101
22	Commit Your Way	106
23	Simplicity and Godly Sincerity	112
24	In Deed and In Truth	117
25	Completion	122
26	Your Example	128
27	His Desires	134
28	Rescue	140
29	He Loves Me	146

Closing Reflection   152

Appendices   155
Appendix 1   Our Schedule   156
Appendix 2   Notes from My Journal   157
Appendix 3   Verses   159
Appendix 4   Balloon Moments   162
Appendix 5   His Desires   163

Small Group Reading Plan and Facilitator's Guide   165

Closing Remarks   171

Bibliography   173

*"Not that I have already obtained this
or am already perfect,
but I press on to make it my own,
because Christ Jesus has made me his own."
Philippians 3:12*

Introduction

This book was completely God's idea. While I was nursing my youngest child one morning in 2017, my mind became unusually quiet. I felt tremendous peace. A moment later, I did not hear an audible voice, but I had a thought that wasn't mine: God whispered to me to write a book to capture my need for His help in motherhood and the practical ways He was instructing me. He wanted me to share that experience with other mothers of young children like myself. He wanted to use my weakness for the glory of His name.

I wrote this book over the course of a little more than three years, with many heartfelt thanks to my husband Jeff for giving me whole days here and there to work on it. I began in 2017 when our youngest, Joel, was nine months old; our middle child, Liza, was 2 years old, and our oldest, Van, was almost 5. As I finish writing it now in 2021, Joel is 4 years old, Liza is 6, and Van is 8.

It is a vulnerable thing to write and publish this book because it captures and distills the hardest challenges I have faced in motherhood over the past three years. On the whole, my family's life is really very wonderful. Our days include a peaceful routine, a stable home life, lots of talk about Jesus, home-cooked meals, lots of reading, biking, Legos, dance parties, art, and much more. We are thankful to God for these endless blessings from Him. But, we are still a family of five, all with fallen natures, and three of us are young children. Because of this, our blessed days also involve varying degrees of noise, conflict, emotion, disobedience, and correction. Our days are not mostly chaotic and I am not usually a bundle of nerves, all thanks to God's grace. But every day there are numerous moments when the responsibilities of motherhood have me actively clinging to Jesus for practical and spiritual direction.

I am willing to share my weaknesses because God told me to and because I know He has a plan to use them. I am also willing to share them because, to my surprise, they are the reason I have come to see what Jesus matters for my everyday mothering life. By facing my own weaknesses, I have gotten to know God in ways I hadn't known were possible. It is exactly because I could not resolve the hardest moments in mothering myself that I found that Jesus matters for every single moment.

I chose to compose this book in a workbook style. As I share about my own moments of need and reliance on Jesus, you can process your own needs and find Jesus ready to speak His satisfying refreshment and life into your everyday moments. God is truly ready to walk hand in hand with us as we raise our young children.

"The Spirit of the Lord God is upon me,
because the Lord has anointed me to bring good news...
to proclaim the year of the Lord's favor...
to grant to those who mourn in Zion...
the garment of praise instead of a faint spirit."
Isaiah 61: 1-3 (selections)

How to Use This Book

Read
This book contains 29 entries. In each entry, I first address you: my friend. Then in each entry, I address God, speaking to Him directly, in the form of a written prayer. I hope you will feel that you are reading a letter from a friend and then reading my prayer journal.

Respond
At the end of each entry you will find two days of questions - three questions per day - to prompt you to grab hold of your own particular faintness of heart and bring it to God to invite Him in. Let me please recommend that you not complete all six questions on an entry at once. Instead, spend the recommended two days to mull over those questions and Bible verses. This way you give each topic your heartfelt reflection, conversation with God about it, and listening ear for how God will respond to you. You will need a Bible with you to complete the questions.

Pray †
Last, follow my prompt to stop and talk with God each day after you complete the response questions.

Grace
I hope you will be patient, generous, and kind with yourself as you imperfectly, but wholeheartedly, cling to Jesus' hand as you mother your children. His work in us is progressive over time. He is the author and perfecter of our faith, as we fix our eyes on Jesus (Hebrews 12:2) and He transforms us gradually, by one degree of glory to another (2 Corinthians 3:18).

As you study and come across a Bible verse that really hits you, please let it get personal. Write it down and post it somewhere you will see it often. God's Word is living and active and it is a powerful means of His giving His love and help to us!

I pray you will find, as I do, that our weaknesses are entry points for taking God's hand and finding that He is already abundantly there and ready for the taking.

An Introductory Prayer

I encourage you to read this prayer out loud as you begin this study. You are seeking God with all your heart, and He promises to be near to us when we seek Him.

> *"You will seek me and find me, when you seek me with all your heart. I will be found by you, declares the Lord."*
> *Jeremiah 29:13-14*

✝

Lord,

I ask You to cause me to trust You so much that I listen for Your direction and follow Your lead as I parent my children. You alone are the way, the truth, and the life. I desire to follow You wholeheartedly and to love my children with Your awesome love.

You designed me to be fulfilled in close relationship with You. You designed me to be full of hope and joy as I walk through life together with You. I say "yes" to that plan of Yours as I mother my children. May my children in turn know and love You and build their lives on You. May they come to share You and Your love with others.

What follows in this workbook, Lord, is my heartfelt endeavor to invite You into my everyday moments and to walk closely with You as I mother my children.

Thank You, Heavenly Father, for Your abundant, overflowing, always-present, never-faltering love for me and for my children. Thank You, Father, for sending Jesus that we may enjoy true life with You both now and forever.

Amen.

~1~
Say "Yes"

September 24, 2017

Dear friend,

My experience is that many mothers feel faint of heart and inadequately equipped for the momentous task of raising their children. While my heart soars in the joys of mothering, the task is often so all-consuming and so multi-faceted. On some days it is defeating. And it is always never-ending! It requires the best of my mind, my soul, and my body, and all of it seemingly all of the time.

There is a saying that "Motherhood is not for the faint of heart." Have you heard that? When I heard it for the first time, I cringed inwardly and I thought to myself, "Oh no! Don't say that! I get very faint of heart!" I didn't like that the saying implies that those who become faint of heart aren't up to the challenge of raising young children. I'm terribly passionate about raising my three very young disciples, about loving them well, and teaching them to follow Jesus. But as a plain old human being, I suffer from becoming fainthearted over it. On particularly hard days, I wonder whether I have what it takes to do it honorably or gladly.

The truth, though, is that mothering *is* for the faint of heart, because God is especially close to us when we are faint of heart and clinging to Him. Psalm 34:18 says that "The Lord is near to the brokenhearted and saves the crushed in spirit". He is present with us; He is encouraging us, teaching us, guiding us, comforting us, even correcting us. I am certainly inadequate for the full task of mothering. In my own strength, I find that it is not possible for me to do it gladly or honorably, however much I wish to. But God, who is the Lord Almighty and the great I Am, acts powerfully and intervenes in my everyday life to show me that in Him I can nurture and train my children in a way that deeply honors Him and brings life.

God participates in our lives, and He does not do it from a distance. God shows Himself truthful, real, and loving, entering into the nitty-gritty details of our lives with us. His care for us is not conceptual; it is practical and present. As we read His Word, as we decide to say "yes" to Him in the little moments of our days, and as we learn to listen for Him guiding us, we experience that He is providing Himself at all times and in every way as we mother our children.

God restores my strength and my joy in motherhood again and again. Not just once and for all on one occasion and then I have all that I need. And not just a few times over the course of my motherhood. He does it all day, every day. He restores me with that frequency and faithfulness because that is how often I become depleted and need Him and because He does not give up or go away. My experience is that Jesus' grace and strength are always there for the taking, always available to me. It is up to me to say "yes" to His offer. In each moment, in my faintness of heart, He is waiting for me to grab hold of Him, to receive His continual offer of Himself. This faith matters in my everyday life, in my every moment. Our faith is more than only believing that He is who He says He is. Faith in Jesus is living in a way that genuinely and actively trusts our messy, everyday moments to Him.

With love,
Lauren

> "Thus says the Lord: Stand by the roads, and look,
> And ask for the ancient paths, where the good way is;
> And walk in it, And find rest for your souls.'"
> Jeremiah 6:16

✝

Lord,

You use even my weaknesses to grow me closer to You and to show me that You are who You say You are. You do not meet me in my weakness and turn away from me; You use my weakness to fix my eyes upon You, my steady rock. Your help is continual. Would you please open the eyes of my heart to see You present and available in ways that are new to me? Use the very real challenges of my everyday mothering to put Yourself radiantly on display to me.

Your Word tells me that all things, including my motherhood and my children's childhood, are for Your glory, so that You will be more known and loved. Please give me rest from emotional weariness as I try to lean on You more and more.

Amen.

Responding:

Day 1

What does the saying "Motherhood is not for the faint of heart" make you think and feel?

_____
_____
_____
_____

Read Psalm 34:4-7 and write verse 5 below. In His kindness, God has turned our attention to Him and we are looking to Him to guide us as we mother our children. What is your reaction to the promise God makes to us in verse 5?

_____
_____
_____
_____

Read Romans 11:36 and write it here. This verse says *all things* are to God and through God. If everything is to God and through God, then that includes our parenting: our parenting is from Him and to Him and through Him. What does it mean to you that your parenting is "to Him"? What does it mean to you that your parenting is "through Him"?

_____
_____
_____
_____

Pray: Read over what you have written down in response to today's questions. Close your eyes now and talk honestly with God about what you have written and about what you are thinking and feeling.

Day 2

Read Psalm 46:1-3 and 10. In verse 10, God instructs us to "Be still, and know that I am God." In what areas of mothering do you want to start letting God take over and lead you?

_____
_____
_____
_____

Read and write Hebrews 12:12. Let it sink in that God realizes that we become weak. He knows that we are in need of Him. That is His design for us. What aspects of mothering make your hands droop or your knees weak? List them here and then offer them to God for healing.

_____
_____
_____
_____

Read and write Isaiah 51:3, and believe the promises God makes to us in this verse. Which part speaks most directly to your needs right now?

_____
_____
_____

Pray: Read over what you have written down in response to today's questions. Close your eyes now and talk honestly with God about what you have written and about what you are thinking and feeling.

> *"Be still, and know that I am God.*
> *I will be exalted among the nations,*
> *I will be exalted in the earth!"*
> *Psalm 46:10*

~2~
He Takes Me by the Hand

October 6, 2017

Dear friend,

I have had a lot of days lately that are so effortful and I am so disappointed in how I've handled various situations with my children that I start to doubt whether I can handle my mothering role terribly respectably. I had always thought that I would be consistently strong and capable as a mom, and so my behavior sometimes surprises me. On these days my weaknesses feel like they are dissipating my vision and passion for motherhood. This thing I feel so utterly passionate about, I discover I'm unable to carry out according to my plan.

Because of His power and kindness, God meets me in the places of my weakness and takes me by the hand. He does not leave me alone and He participates far more than I know to ask (Ephesians 3:20). I see Him do this in two main ways in my everyday life:

- <u>God hears my weak cries to Him and extends abundantly more help to me than I deserve.</u>

- <u>At other times, God sees my failure to follow Him and He invites me onward anyway.</u>

When you ask, He will do the same for you.

<u>God hears my weak cries to Him and extends abundantly more help to me than I deserve.</u> Dozens of times every day, I try to quiet my mind in the midst of somebody's tantrum or refusal to go to his room as I have told him to. In those moments, the noise of the tantrum, or the simultaneity of my children's voices needing me, or a continuing cry feels like it sets off loud sirens in my mind. I try to quiet my thoughts because I become so faint of heart in the midst of those moments. I feel overwhelmed, and I want to handle it lovingly, but I feel frustrated that we find ourselves here again. I am trying so hard to handle those messy situations God's way, but still I feel that I am in far over my head. I close my eyes and say to God, "Lord, I need You in this moment, and not me". I'm praying because I'm tapped out and I need God to show up so that I, with anger and frustration, do not.

Earlier this week, for example, my oldest erupted into an emotional tantrum in response to my having told him to use the bathroom and wash his hands before lunch. It was a simple, usual request. Transition times are consistently the hardest for him, so it was not surprising to hear him become upset, but it was still so utterly frustrating. I walked over to Van in the doorway to our powder room and opened my mouth. To my great surprise, quite miraculously, something gentle and thoughtful came out. In a whisper! What I heard myself saying was not what I had been feeling or had planned to say. Crouching down to look him in the eyes, I heard myself say to my son, "This is not the way". I had recently read Jesus' gentle correction to Peter in the Garden of Gethsemane and God brought it to mind in that moment (Lloyd-Jones 2007). In response, Van crumbled into my arms - a far cry from the wild, loud moment before. His tantrum was over. I was taken aback and realized that the Holy Spirit had met me in the middle of the moment. He had me say something that I hadn't planned to. He inserted Himself into that moment. He was there in action!

God surprised me in a similar way just yesterday: I had told my daughter Liza to go into the bathroom and she had not. My first inclination was to reprimand her. Instead, I picked her up and brought her silently into the bathroom, sitting her down gently on her kiddie potty and leading her through the motions without a reprimand. The tension of the moment dissipated. She hugged my knees from beside the potty, twice! We were able to go on to a peaceful lunch afterwards. I hadn't decided to handle that situation in the way that I did. I was surprised to find myself treating her so kindly in the midst of my inner frustration. I sensed that it was God who had had me do it that way. It was as if He held my tongue for me and as if He gave me His gentle hands in place of my natural inclination. Philippians 2:13 says that "it is God who works in you, both to will and to work for his good pleasure". I experienced that to be true: He acted through me; He motivated me to choose His way.

In addition to my surprise at experiencing God's help to me in such practical ways in real time, I was equally floored by how immediately and compliantly my children responded to Him in those moments. His gentle, loving way was compelling. It stood out and grabbed their attention. God used my children's tantrums and my sudden inability in the face of them to surprise us all with His sudden provision.

<u>In moments that appear less successful, God sees my failure to follow Him well, and He invites me onward anyway</u>. I consider my "less successful" moments in motherhood to be those in which I want to treat my children lovingly, but I fail to. Emotions get the better of me and I step out of God's way, acting apart from His instructions to love my kids extravagantly. I've shouted at them or handled them harshly.

Afterwards, I apologize, disappointed that I've given them those loud emotions instead of giving them God. I tell them that I stepped outside of God's instructed way to us. I help them see that I disobeyed God in that moment. It is crystal clear to all of us in those moments whose way is better: mine or God's. When I have had to apologize, God shines brightly against my wrongdoings and disobedience. We all see that His way is more life-giving and more full of love than ours is naturally.

And then, like the sun breaking through the clouds, my children forgive me readily and immediately and I am stunned by the love God pours out on me despite my not deserving it. I've behaved unlovably but God loves me through my children anyway. Through them, He invites me onward. I am humbled to receive such kindness and mercy from God.

God shows Himself present and real and active with me - when I fall into step with Him and also when I don't. In both kinds of moments, I am in need of Him. He meets me and takes me by the hand either way - when I cooperate and when I don't. He willingly bears my weaknesses and my failings. Undeterred by my stumbling ability to mother with His love, He draws me further onward in His good and kind plans. God participates with me in my everyday life.

With love,
Lauren

> "Fear not, for I am with you;
> be not dismayed, for I am your God;
> I will strengthen you, I will help you,
> I will uphold you with my righteous right hand."
> Isaiah 41:10

✝

Lord,

Whether You surprise me in my weakness with Your provision, or I let my emotions win and step outside of Your way, You are present and active in the details of my mothering days and moments. I am Yours and You are here with me. I keep seeing You meet me right here, repeatedly restoring the strength and joy I need and find only in You. You are in my corner as I mother my children and You do not shy away from offering Your strength in the hardest moments. My passion for loving my children Your way is Your passion, too. You will be glorified in this family.

Thank You, Lord, that Your power and Your kindness are so immense that You take me by the hand and lead me onward in Your good plans in such undeniably personal ways. You do not only say that You love me; You show me that You love me. You do not leave me on my own and in my weakness. You enter into my daily life with me. Your love is unfathomably deep towards me.

Amen.

Responding:

Day 1

In what way do you relate to being passionate about loving your kids while also being aware of your shortcomings to do it well?

_____
_____
_____
_____

Read Psalm 138:2-3 and write verse 3. In what specific part(s) of your day today would you benefit from calling on God to strengthen you?

_____
_____
_____
_____

Read and write 2 Corinthians 4:7. Thinking back, have you experienced a time when God took you by the hand and helped you so much that you knew it was His doing? Describe that time.

_____
_____
_____
_____

Pray: Read over what you have written down in response to today's questions. Close your eyes now and talk honestly with God about what you have written and about what you are thinking and feeling.

Day 2
Read Psalm 25:4-5 and 12-13. Write verse 12. Yesterday you listed a part or two of your day during which you could benefit from calling on God to strengthen you. How will you speak and behave differently in those moments if you decide to let God lead you in them?

_____
_____
_____
_____

God is changing us as we spend time with Him both in prayer and Bible study and in the middle of our everyday life with Him. Read and write 2 Corinthians 3:18. What is an area of your mothering that you are in need of God to transform?

_____
_____
_____
_____

Read Revelation 21:6-7 and write those verses here. God knows that we are faint of heart; he calls us "thirsty". He gives us access to the spring of the water of spiritual life: Himself. He wants us to "conquer" as we rely on Him in the challenges of life. What do you think "conquering" could look like for you as a mother?

_____
_____
_____

Pray: Read over what you have written down in response to today's questions. Close your eyes now and talk honestly with God about what you have written and about what you are thinking and feeling.

> *"On the day I called, you answered me;*
> *my strength of soul you increased."*
> *Psalm 138:3*

~3~
For the Glory of His Name

November 13, 2017

Dear friend,

For most of my life, my faith has consisted of waiting for God to act in my life according to what I had asked and envisioned. He was relevant to my daily life to the extent that He answered my prayers in the way I asked Him to. I knew that God is wiser than I am and that He may choose to answer "no" to my prayers. But for many years, the strength of my belief in His personal love for me depended on how well I considered my life to be going. In retrospect, I see that my faith revolved around me.

Over the past ten or so years, though, as I have been taught to read my Bible searchingly and as I have had opportunities to study and discuss it with other women following Jesus, I have begun to relate to God differently. Now, I do not relate to God as only the giver of blessings. Now I have a personal, daily relationship with Him and it is not based upon what I receive from Him. Now I believe God because I see Him continually at work in my life and in the world in ways consistent with who He says He is, not with what I ask of Him. I am not waiting for Him to agree to my perspective or my terms; now, I get to align my life with where He is at work. I get to join Him in His ways. He is now the focal point of my faith.

I am leaning on God and walking with Him in my everyday life now. I find that He is always merciful, always gracious, and always gentle. In all circumstances - through my hardest mothering moments, through my joyful mothering moments, through my unexpected mothering moments - He is present, active, and full of love. All of His ways reveal His glory, His unmatched magnificence. Living closely with Him, now I can see that literally everything works to the glory of His name. Everything points to Him and His goodness, including the hardest parts of this fallen world that show how much better He is.

God opened my eyes to see Him at work in all things, and now I want to live for the sake of His being made much of (Piper 2000). I desire to walk closely together with God and to let Him use my life to display His matchless glory (Sjogren 2003). (Thank You, Lord, for those who have taught me!) As a mother, God has given me the special opportunity to make Him known to my children. I want them to learn that they, too, will find real spiritual life in Him alone.

And so my life, including mothering now, moment by moment, is about letting God have His way in me. I get to turn to God in His power and love all throughout the day. As I rely on Him, we see Him even more than before. My life can increasingly magnify Him.

A motherhood situation from earlier this week will help to illustrate: My energetic, insistent 5-year-old came into the kitchen to tell me something during our independent quiet time one afternoon, despite my instructions not to do so. For years now I've required the clear boundary of a quiet time for us every day between 2:45 and 4:00 p.m. I expect him to play in the front room and stay there. I spend my time in the kitchen and family room. At 4:00 p.m. daily, I come for him and can again give him my full, loving attention for a few minutes before we return to the day refreshed. I really need my quiet time as a respite of peace after a long morning of being together, answering questions, sorting out disagreements, and juggling needs.

As I saw Van approaching me during quiet time earlier this week, the decision I faced was this: How do I uphold my good conviction to protect our quiet time, while giving him God and not my anger and frustration? I knew I must turn him away because he has to learn that quiet time is truly that; I knew that to receive one question would only mean he would continue to bring me others all throughout the (no longer) "quiet" time. But how do I do that in a God-honoring way?, I wondered. I felt burnt out from the morning and frustrated that he was interrupting my hour of peace and disobeying my clear instruction. I wanted so much to uphold my expectation without being mean-spirited about it. I knew how I *wanted* to handle it but my emotions of the moment clamored to get out!

In those few seconds leading up to that exchange with my son, as Van walked across the room to me, God quietly whispered to my heart, instructing me to be at once loving and clear. He was calling me to sacrifice my emotions for the sake of His name. He wanted me to do it His way. To do that, He said, I must be loving and clear. Equally. Not loving now, and then clear later, by engaging him for a few minutes and then sending him back on his way. Not clear now, and then loving later, by harshly sending him away now and then fixing it later with kindness. No. I must reply with a tone and words that are both loving and clear all at once. Right now.

God held the defining key for me in that moment, and I believed Him. To live like I believed Him, I knew I had to follow through on what He'd said to do. The struggle to actually do that required so much self-control! I looked up at Van briefly, and with an unexpressive, peaceful face told him that I would come and see him at 4:00 p.m. I immediately turned my eyes back down to my Bible and journal. I had to keep my head down so as not to watch for a reaction or give him the impression that I was doing so! He stood and voiced his thought a few different ways for a minute or so, and I remained unresponsive. He returned to the front room. He was disappointed, yes, but he didn't feel unloved. He just knew that it had not been the right time for an interaction. A few minutes later I slowly looked up to be sure he had gone and stayed. He had! I smiled! What a serious accomplishment of walking hand in hand with God. Without God's prompting, or my obedience, the moment would have looked very differently than it did.

Actually doing what God has said to do involves dying to myself and choosing His way instead (Romans 6:11). It doesn't mean I will necessarily receive a stellar response from my son or a quiet time without further interruption (although those are blessings I readily and gladly accept with thanks!). But by giving my son God's way instead of my own natural one, I say "yes" to God's design and "yes" to His hand at work in our lives. It is a tremendous blessing to say "yes" to God in my hard moments and to find that, as He promises, He truly is the way.

I ask God to cause His good guidance to me to eclipse any emotion in me that stands in the way of His glory. May I choose Him in our everyday moments.

With love,
Lauren

> "And your ears shall hear a word behind you saying, 'This is the way, walk in it,' when you turn to the right or when you turn to the left."
>
> Isaiah 30:21

✝

Lord,

My prayer today, my heart crying out within me today, is "Lord, I want to choose You and Your way all day long." I don't want only to understand Your way; I don't want only to hear Your instruction; I want to do what You have said. I want to mother kindly, gently, full of love and compassion, and also clearly, undistracted and undeterred from Your way.

The trouble is that I am truly weak; I feel my faintheartedness. I need You, Lord, to flood my spirit with Yourself. Teach me about living for Your glory. Teach me clearly so that I can follow You. Motivate me to say "yes" to You, I ask.

Amen.

Responding:

Day 1

When are you challenged to be both loving and clear with your children? When is it hardest for you to hold the line? How do you feel in those moments?

_____
_____
_____
_____

Read and write John 3:30 here. How should this verse impact the way we parent our children?

_____
_____
_____
_____

Read and write Psalm 67:1-3. What does this passage teach you about one of the reasons God shows us His ways?

_____
_____
_____
_____

Pray: Read over what you have written down in response to today's questions. Close your eyes now and talk honestly with God about what you have written and about what you are thinking and feeling.

Day 2
God's design is that we need Him, cling to Him, and rely on Him. Read Psalm 119:31-32 and write verse 32. What do you notice about how God influences our ability to follow Him?

_____
_____
_____
_____

The Bible tells us that God's ultimate victory over all things has already been secured. Read and write Revelation 11:17. "To reign" means to possess ultimate authority and to exercise it. What will it mean for God to reign in your mothering?

_____
_____
_____
_____

Read 1 Kings 19:11-13. Notice in verse 12 that God spoke in the sound of a low whisper. Have you ever experienced God whispering to you about mothering? Are you willing to pray and ask God to quiet your heart so you can hear His guiding whispers?

_____
_____
_____
_____

Pray: Read over what you have written down in response to today's questions. Close your eyes now and talk honestly with God about what you have written and about what you are thinking and feeling.

"He must increase, but I must decrease."
John 3:30

~4~
Love of Christ

December 1, 2017

Dear friend,

Do you find, like I do, that the way your children behave heavily influences how you mother that day?

For one thing, I find that my mood is often determined by how closely my children have obeyed me. I am more cheerful and buoyant when they are operating according to my expectations. I am more brooding and frustrated when they are not meeting my expectations. While the difference there is a natural and human one, the truth is that regardless of the contents of the day, the Lord is supposed to be my steady guide. My mood need not fluctuate so dramatically. My status in Christ has not changed and so my state need not either.

I also find that I will often let my children's behavior determine how I order our day. I will focus so much on managing my children's behavior that I will sacrifice parts of our day that they would not be amenable to.

Additionally, I find that at times I give my children my love and attention only to the extent that I feel they have earned it. I will speak in a loving voice to them or touch them lovingly according to how lovable I feel they have been.

But the life God offers and actively pours into me is not dependent on what I have given Him. (Thank You, Lord!) His faithfulness towards me does not operate out of the degree of His satisfaction with my obedience. No, He loves me steadily because He is mine and I am His. His love in action towards me does not hinge on how lovably I have behaved. Rather, His love chases me down; He loves me when I am unlovable and full of sin (Romans 5:8). He is unchanging and unflappable in His love for me. His kindness towards me actually leads me to repentance (Romans 2:4). He sustains His loving ways towards me no matter what.

God's consistent and faithful love towards me no matter what is the reason for any joy, any strength, any hope, and any peace that I have. His faithfulness towards me is the reason I have joy and strength, and hope and peace, to give to the people in my life. If I want my children to enjoy joy, strength, hope, and peace, mustn't they receive the consistent and faithful love of Christ that provides it? And who on this earth is better positioned to love them in action but me, their mother?

I desire with all my heart for my parenting to be controlled not by my children's fluctuating behavior or lovability but rather by the steady, unrelenting love of Christ. I want to love my children with that kind of love.

I want Jesus to drive what I say and how I say it. I want His steady love to drive how gently I touch my children and how generously I respond to their needs. I want to operate daily out of the abundance of love with which He regularly covers and comforts me.

God sees this desire of mine and in response, He is kindly teaching me, in each little flare-up behavior moment of my children's days, to hold off for just a moment. In that first moment that He holds me back, He allows me to watch my children, quietly and perceptively. He is teaching me to hold back the emotions I feel flying to the surface in the face of my children's less desirable moments. He is allowing me to remember His love for them in those moments.

Actively remembering God's love for my children in those harder moments, I am able to perceive more of their hearts and not just their behavior (Tripp 1995). Perceiving my children with a heart full of love, I can better appreciate where they are coming from and what is contributing to their behavior. Before I consider consequences, I can have empathy even alongside parental wisdom. Are they in need of a hug?, I ask myself. Do they need guidance to go play alone quietly for a few minutes? Are they overwrought and need to sit down with their blanket and a book? Certainly there are plenty of times that consequences for behavior will still be required, but looking at them through God's eyes of love, no matter what the situation requires of me, I can do it from a place of His steady love.

The key to being able to perceive my children with God's love, and to respond to them with it, lies in my being genuinely satisfied myself by God's love for me. It requires me to be so confident of God's love for me and so transformed by His love, that every day and all day I return again and again to resting in His love. Slowing down to take His hand, emotions do not need to control me; the love of Christ can.

With love,
Lauren

"The love of Christ controls us."
2 Corinthians 5:14

✝

Lord,

Please bubble up to the surface of me so that when I open my mouth in those challenging moments when one of my children is crying again, I will let You live in me (2 Corinthians 5:15). I want to respond to their upsetting moments not with exasperation but instead with Your gentle direction and wisdom. I want to see their hearts and address those heart needs, not only the behavior manifestations of them.

And even as I say that, Lord, give me Your wisdom to discern when compassion and comfort is appropriate, and, on the other hand, when firmer correction is called for. I need Your discernment right in the midst of those moments. I want to respond with Your love by giving them what is best for them, even when that involves discipline.

Lord, it comes easily to me to want to correct my children when how they behave doesn't align with what I've taught them. The discrepancy between what they've done and what they've been taught to do can be so clear to me. But I also want to maintain high hopes for them, anticipating that You are in fact bringing them along in Your ways. I want to watch for the plans You already have working for my children and through my children and so send them lovingly and helpfully along that way. I want to see them with Your eyes full of hope and love and the good news that You are leading them on Your path of life. Cause me to treat them with the eyes of faith that You give me, with the love You intend for them.

Amen.

Responding:

Day 1

God is the ultimate example for us as we uphold our expectations for our children while extending great warmth to them. Read Luke 15:21-24 and write verse 21. How could the father's example in this passage influence your parenting today?

_____

_____

_____

Read Isaiah 55:1-3 and see that God invites us to come to Him empty-handed. His love is not earned or paid for. Write verse 1. What is one practical way you could express to your children that they do not need to earn your love?

_____

_____

Read and write Isaiah 12:1. We can learn from God's example to turn away from our anger and instead see our children's need for comfort and love. Name a moment in your days that is typically angering for you. How specifically can you plan to turn away from anger in that moment and instead extend comfort and love to your child, even if it involves disciplining him?

Pray: Read over what you have written down in response to today's questions. Close your eyes now and talk honestly with God about what you have written and about what you are thinking and feeling.

Day 2
Read Colossians 3:12 and write it here. For which virtue(s) do you need God's powerful help this week? Why in particular do you need it?

Read Ephesians 4:29-32 and write down the verse or words from that passage that most strike a chord with you today.

God wants to fill us with expectant hopes for our children. Read and write Romans 15:13. How do you need God to grow your hope for your children? Do you need Him to fill you with deeper joy or peace as you trust Him with that area of parenting? Talk with God and tell Him your needs.

_____

_____

_____

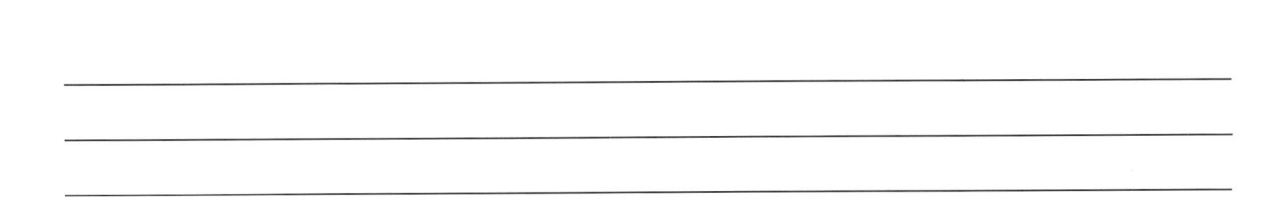

_____

Pray: Read over what you have written down in response to today's questions. Close your eyes now and talk honestly with God about what you have written and about what you are thinking and feeling.

> "For it is God who works in you,
> both to will and to work
> for his good pleasure."
> Philippians 2:13

~5~
Follow

January 21, 2018

Dear friend,

God has been speaking a lot to me about waiting a moment before reacting to my children, particularly in tougher moments with them when my tendency would be to become frustrated. He extended the concept recently, giving me a thought that I didn't think of myself. It was like a quiet whisper to my soul, not audible, but perceptible nonetheless. It was this: instead of immediately reacting to the challenges that arise in my days, I can quiet down in the middle of those moments, pause, *watch to see where the Holy Spirit goes, and then follow Him there.* It was like God tuned the eyes of my heart into a radio station that had been on all along without my having noticed it.

I first perceived the idea when my daughter Liza, gentle and concerned, noticed the rushed way I was tackling situations as they arose. She asked me, "Mommy, why are you going quickly?" Liza is slow and peaceful by deep nature. I am often bustling and multi-tasking. Being so different from me in that way, she has pointed out to me on several occasions how unnecessary my hustle is, in the form of that question. How gracious of God to point this out to me through my gentle, loving daughter.

God caught my attention through those repeated interactions with Liza as I hurried to get through one task, one challenge, and on to the next. It felt like God suggested to me that I try doing everything slowly and intentionally, and to see how that changed my perspective and even helped improve the circumstances. To do everything about a half step "too slow" by my usual standard. It was counter to my tendency. Tired of my unrelenting pace and eager to allow God further into our day, I agreed and tried it out. Liza loved it! She gave me lots of extra, sweet smiles. I never let on to my kids that I was doing anything any differently on purpose.

Slowing down, I discovered that I could nearly "see" the Holy Spirit going a step ahead of me: I could notice my kids' challenges and emotional uprisings, perceive how the Spirit would have me enter in, and then follow Him there. And "there" was a far different place from where I, in my own limitations and frustrations, tend naturally to take things.

I am finding that as I follow the Holy Spirit, I am freed up from making as many managing decisions as I had been making. I am freed up from my sense of needing to talk my kids through the day in an effort to manage it all. Instead, I can watch to see God's lead and then go there myself. He has never once misguided any of us!

One evening in particular, I was cooking dinner and asking Him to help me to go more slowly and deliberately about my responsibilities. I was overseeing the kids' playtime, finishing up dinner, tidying up from the late afternoon, and folding laundry. Dinner was almost finished; all was in the oven. I felt very busy, and the ambient noise of the kids playing nearby added to my sense of busyness. But I was asking God to slow me down in the midst of it all. I surprised myself by sitting down on our comfy chair to relax a moment or two instead of jumping to the next to-do. What a breath of fresh air that was! It was so out of character and it made me smile to see myself do it. That was certainly God's prompting. I felt so comforted when I realized He could use my simply sitting down as a way to have me follow His lead. I noticed that my children were all playing happily and appropriately. Peacefully, I enjoyed observing them without joining in. It was a rare choice for me to simply watch for a moment, not pushing on to the next task nor joining in. It was wonderful to simply be their at-peace mother in that moment.

God had me sense His presence vividly in that moment. He had slowed me down to the point of relaxing before dinner, and here I was, trusting *Him to do the doing with my children*. He let me see that He had already been present with my children without me jumping in to manage them. God let me sense *His presence* being enough for the circumstances. He was causing me to dwell in His shadow (Psalm 91:1). It was a profound moment. I actually felt enveloped in His presence. I had the sensation that oil or candle wax was running warmly over the crown of my head and to my neck and shoulders and down my sides. His presence was nearly tangible in that way. He was really quieting me and I was blessed to let Him be peacefully at work in my home.

Letting God teach me, listening for His quiet direction, I can take hold of God's hand and follow Him as He is at work. His presence is surely with us all the time. I pray He opens the eyes of my heart to perceive and follow Him regularly!

With love,
Lauren

> *"For my thoughts are not your thoughts, neither are your ways my ways, declares the Lord. For as the heavens are higher than the earth, so are my ways higher than your ways and my thoughts than your thoughts."*
> **Isaiah 55:8**

✝

Lord,

Thank You that You see my desire to follow You and You meet me exactly where I am. You met me in a moment when I remembered Your instruction to me to slow down and to follow You, and even though I was struggling to do it, You guided me gently and yet deliberately.

I stand in awe of You that You can so quickly enter into the middle of a wound-up moment and change my perspective completely. You gave me Your wisdom and then You used a specific moment to weave Your better ways into my everyday life. I am so grateful for Your personal, loving care.

Amen.

Responding:

Day 1

Do you ever sense that you unintentionally rob a moment of its fullness by rushing through it? Which moments do you tend to rush through? List them out here so that you become aware of opportunities to watch for God's glory at work in those everyday moments.

_____
_____
_____
_____

Read and write Isaiah 30:21. When could you sit down today and watch to see how God is already at work in your home? Commit to sitting there without distraction for four full minutes and talk with God at the end of your time. What does He impress upon you during that time?

_____
_____
_____
_____

Read and write Galatians 5:25. In what way(s) do you think you are feeling the Holy Spirit direct you as you mother?

_____
_____
_____
_____

Pray: Read over what you have written down in response to today's questions. Close your eyes now and talk honestly with God about what you have written and about what you are thinking and feeling.

Day 2

Read and write Psalm 36:7-9 and write verse 7. Think of a moment in your days that is often overwhelming or upsetting. How do you usually feel in that moment? How would you feel differently if you let yourself hide in the shadow of God's wings in that moment?

_____
_____
_____
_____

Read Jeremiah 31:10-14 and write verse 12 here. Close your eyes and imagine yourself being "radiant over the goodness of the Lord". List 12 reasons you have today to be "radiant over the goodness of God"; these can be truths about God or details from your life. Your list of reasons to be thankful to God shows you that He is living and active in your everyday life.

_____
_____
_____
_____

Read Psalm 112:1-2 and write verse 2. Notice that as we are faithful to Him, He promises something to us. What does He promise?

_____

_____

_____

_____

Pray: Read over what you have written down in response to today's questions. Close your eyes now and talk honestly with God about what you have written and about what you are thinking and feeling.

> "How precious is your steadfast love, O God!
> The children of mankind take refuge
> in the shadow of your wings."
> Psalm 36:7

~6~
Be Strong

February 4, 2018

Dear friend,

On days when I am feeling weak and like I simply don't have it in me to mother gracefully, all day long I remind myself to hold my very human self to a high standard, to God's standard. I remind myself not to mother out of my emotions but instead out of trust in God that He is at work and that His way works. I have a phrase that I say to myself on those weaker days, and I have it written on a sticky note and posted to my fridge. The note reads:

Be strong and immovable, always abounding in the loving work of the Lord.

It is a paraphrase of God's instruction to us from 1 Corinthians 16:13 and 2 Corinthians 9:8. I've underlined here the words from each of those verses that I pulled out and combined to form the phrase I posted to my fridge:

"Be watchful, stand firm in the faith, act like men, <u>be strong</u>.
Let all that you do be done <u>in love</u>."
1 Corinthians 16:13

"And God is able to make all grace <u>abound</u> to you,
so that having <u>all</u> sufficiency in <u>all</u> things at <u>all</u> times,
you may abound in <u>every good work</u>."
2 Corinthians 9:8

Again, pulling from those two verses, I formed the phrase: *Be strong and immovable, always abounding in the loving work of the Lord.* When I say this phrase out loud to myself, I encourage myself to choose to follow Him when it's hardest.

<u>*Be strong and immovable:*</u>
Be strong, I tell myself! Choose it, that is. Not *feel* strong. Rather, do it. Be strong. Those two words alone are an effective call to arms for me as I speak to my soul in the hard mothering moments, when I am feeling in over my head. I am called to live out the deep life there is in being certain of God's sovereignty over us and at work in all things. He is genuinely more powerful and lasting than the physical circumstances in front of me. When it is hard not to be overcome by the

circumstances, I want to press into my faith and live it out. It requires living out of the strength of my convictions and not my emotions. I know I can trust that God is molding my children into God-following, compassionate, able, independent individuals - even when circumstances tell me we are far off as of yet. I will choose to be strong even now because the joy of the Lord is my strength (Nehemiah 8:10).

...always abounding in the loving...:

Be strong 'in the *loving* work of the Lord', I remind myself. Again, *loving*. I am not representing Jesus or carrying out His purposes when I am mothering with a scowl on my face because "I know best" and "I'm disappointed" in them. I am to mother lovingly...in a loving manner! Sometimes that looks like characteristic love, full of affection and nicknames and special moments. But at other times, I remind myself, love takes the form of good teaching and gentle but firm correction. In love, I am to impose consequences for wrong choices my children have made. As I teach them to obediently follow God's ways, I am loving them well. I want the best for them and I am lovingly showing them the way.

...work of the Lord:

In God's kindness towards us, there are so many parts of motherhood from which we get to derive pleasure, value, and purpose. But nevertheless, much of motherhood is *work* - which by definition means it will be strenuous, vigorous, and effortful. So my work in parenting can many times feel like exactly that - work! And that is okay, that is part of God's plan! I can't expect raising children to be easy, that they would fall into line because I *wish* their hearts' tendencies and their choices a certain way. It is *work* to participate in the long-term transformation that God is bringing about in my children's hearts, and I am privileged that He trusts my part to me.

God also calls me to "work out my salvation in fear and trembling" (Philippians 2:12), truly *working* at sticking to His instruction as I walk closely with Him and teach my children to do the same. I must not only follow God in my thoughts and intentions. I must walk closely with God in what I say and in what I do. That takes great effort on my part. I am called to "love the Lord [my] God with all [my] heart, soul, mind, and strength" (Deuteronomy 6:5). God is not asking for what I can easily give Him. He seeks all of us, all of our strength in going hand in hand with Him. I must move beyond intention to really and truly walk together with Him. God uses His Word to lead us on His path of life.

With love,
Lauren

"Your word is a lamp to my feet and a light to my path...
I am severely afflicted; give me life, Lord,
according to your word!"
Psalm 119:105, 107

✝

Lord,

Thank You that Your words, provided to us in the Bible, matter very much for everyday life. Thank You that as I turn to You for direction, Your Word truly is a lamp to my feet and a light to my path. When I am in the middle of a challenging time, in the middle of "darkness", feeling unequipped to address the challenge before me, please bring to my mind Your words that equip me. You arm me with portions of Your Word that You cause to jump off of the page to me and to serve as my marching orders. As a mother I do at times feel "severely afflicted". Give me life, Lord, according to Your Word!

Would You please remind me in my mothering to be strong and to do everything with Your love? Would you please cause me to be so full of You that I do have all sufficiency in all things at all times to abound in the good work I do for You? Thank You that You hear every one of my words and that You abound in kindness, mercy, and grace towards me as I work to walk with You. Lord, I need You. I love You.

Amen!

Responding:

Day 1
Read Psalm 43:3-5, in which King David is speaking to his soul and calling himself up to a higher standard than his nature tends toward. Write down verse 5 and underline the word "hope". Then read out loud to your own soul what you wrote down, encouraging your soul not to operate out of your emotions but instead out of your trust in God.

_____
_____
_____

Memorize my reminder phrase or write one of your own, so you can speak it out loud to your soul in the middle of the hardest moments when you are feeling weak and unable to do it God's way. Look back over the verses from the past few days if you need inspiration for which verse will help you take God's hand in the messier moments. Write the verse or your reminder phrase on a sticky note and put it on your fridge or over your kitchen sink today. Don't worry about it being pretty - just get it up there, and use it!

_____
_____
_____
_____

Read Hebrews 4:16 and write it here. Tell God about a parenting moment from today when you were not strong or abounding in His loving work. Tell Him how you mishandled it and ask Him for His forgiveness. Receive His mercy and grace to go forward, now free from that moment, and again holding tightly to Him.

_____
_____
_____
_____

Pray: Read over what you have written down in response to today's questions. Close your eyes now and talk honestly with God about what you have written and about what you are thinking and feeling.

Day 2
Read Isaiah 45:22-25 and write the first half of verse 24. What have you previously relied on for your strength, other than God? Write your answer here so that you can leave those things behind as sources of your strength, knowing that only in the Lord will you find true righteousness and strength to mother His way.

_____
_____
_____
_____

Read James 4:5-8 and write verse 6. We are "humble" when we know we cannot do it on our own and we deeply perceive our need for Him to be alive in us. Is there a way you tend to think or act that you need to humbly turn away from?

_____
_____

_____

_____

Read 2 Corinthians 4:7-11 and write verse 11. What does it mean to you for Jesus' life to be "manifested" in your life?

_____

_____

_____

_____

Pray: Read over what you have written down in response to today's questions. Close your eyes now and talk honestly with God about what you have written and about what you are thinking and feeling.

> *"But the one who looks into the perfect law, the law of liberty, and perseveres, being no hearer who forgets but a doer who acts, he will be blessed in his doing."*
> *James 1:25*

~7~
Glad and Confident

February 19, 2018

Dear friend,

When I stop and think objectively about all of the very real challenges of mothering and the things that frustrate me the most, I realize that I don't have to let them drive me. I don't have to allow them to make me "go there". In the midst of them, those moments feel so powerful. But in reality they pale in comparison to the present spiritual reality of God's work in our hearts and in our lives.

This is terribly significant and worthy of our attention! Instead of being troubled, I can be glad about the decisions I make as I parent my children. I can be glad - actually and truly glad - not just trying to be glad in the midst of it all. God guides me as I mother my children, and I can truly rest in that. "Be glad in the Lord, and rejoice, O righteous, and shout for joy, all you upright in heart!" (Psalm 32:11). Because I am relying on Jesus, I can have genuine joy in mothering!

I can be genuinely confident, too, in the expectations that I have for my children. I don't have to join my kids in the disappointment they feel in response to my expectations and my resolve to uphold them. Even when they do not realize it, my high expectations for them provide a needed boundary and bring real blessing to their lives. "In the fear of the Lord one has strong confidence, and his children will have a refuge" (Proverbs 14:26). I am showing them how to live out God's good instruction for them, and in that I can be sure-footed (Proverbs 1:7).

There are moments in parenting that I sense God giving me an idea for a specific activity to do with my kids. At other times, a specific verse will come to mind that is useful to me in instructing or correcting one of them. In those moments, for me it comes relatively easily to be glad and confident as I follow Jesus in my parenting.

But there are plenty of other moments when God has not marked my path forward quite as distinctly, and I have to apply the general wisdom He has given me to the situation at hand. In His kindness, God is beginning to allow me to feel genuinely glad and confident in how I apply His more general wisdom to our everyday life. And that feels like His stamp of approval on my decisions!

So I am glad and confident, for example, when recent days indicate that if I want to get my bathrooms clean, my kids will have to have some down time each alone in their rooms. They would rather be together, but wisdom tells me that would probably result in some difficult interactions requiring my intervention. I know that they aren't used to being split up so that I can work, and I know that they won't really like it. And so that is exactly where I have to decide to be glad and confident. I can either choose to feel badly when they react sadly to my plan, or I can gladly choose to go with the plan that God's wisdom led me to choose and to find freedom in that. By choosing what I know is best, according to my God-given instinct, I get to welcome them into life lived under God's wisdom (Proverbs 4:3-6).

I am starting to feel so much freedom as a mother now because I see that I do not have to dwell in the circumstances that arise when my child bucks up against an expectation I have for him. Because I am following God's guidance, I am confident and content that I am choosing, in love, what is best for my child, to the best of my inspired ability.

With love,
Lauren

> "Enter through the narrow gate.
> For wide is the gate and broad is the road
> that leads to destruction,
> and many enter through it.
> But small is the gate and narrow the road
> that leads to life,
> and only a few find it."
> Matthew 7:13-14

✝

Lord,

I have learned that You know what is best for us, even when we as Your children do not. Your boundaries are not restrictions. You set us on the narrow path for Your glory and our good.

Lord, help me to take action on Your Word, to use Your wisdom to arrange our day and to set appropriate boundaries for my own children. And would you give me confidence and even certainty that I am making the right decisions as I do so? Would you help me to feel so settled in Your guidance to me that I can feel rested and glad to follow through with my plans? I do not want to falter in the face of my children's resistance. Help me to see, with clarity, resolve, and love that, like Your boundaries, the ones I set for my children are for their holiness and ultimately their own happiness in You. Your Word says that "in [Christ] are hidden all the treasures of wisdom and knowledge" (Colossians 2:2-3), and I experience the truth of Your Word. All wisdom is found in You! Please help me apply it to the fabric of our family life.

Amen.

Responding:

Day 1

I often have the sense as a mom that I know what the right boundary or expectation to set for my children is, but I get scared that it will feel too restrictive for them. In what area of life do you struggle to be confident or glad in the expectations you set for your children?

___

___

___

___

God is the source of our motherly instinct and our wisdom to know what our children need, such as a regular naptime and healthy foods. What is a specific expectation that you have wanted to put in place for your children but that you've been afraid to express or to uphold? Will you say "yes" to that prompting from God today and implement it?

___

___

___

___

Thank God right now that as we follow Him, we receive life abundantly. Write down Jesus' words recorded in John 10:10. What does having "life abundantly" mean to you?

___

___

___

___

Pray: Read over what you have written down in response to today's questions. Close your eyes now and talk honestly with God about what you have written and about what you are thinking and feeling.

Day 2

As we follow God's direction to us, we really do feel glad. Read John 15:10-11 and write verse 11. Do you sense that there are any promptings ("commandments") from God about your parenting that you have ignored up to this point? He gives us such joy in following Him closely.

_____
_____
_____
_____

All throughout God's Word, He provides us with instruction on how to live. He uses it to mold us and to direct us. Read and write Psalm 119:105. Is God illuminating for you a change He wants to make in your confidence to set and uphold expectations for your children? Make notes and be specific so that you can turn His prompting into a plan.

_____
_____
_____
_____

Read Psalm 119:33-37 and write verse 37. What are the "worthless" fears or worries that keep you from setting and upholding a high standard for your children? Then, fill in the blanks in the sentences below to help you identify what stands in the way.

_____
_____
_____
_____

I have not held the line in the area of _____ with my children because I am afraid that _____.

I have not held the line in the area of _____ with my children because I worry that _____.

Pray: Read over what you have written down in response to today's questions. Close your eyes now and talk honestly with God about what you have written and about what you are thinking and feeling.

> "And the ransomed of the Lord shall return
> and come to Zion with singing;
> everlasting joy shall be upon their heads;
> they shall obtain gladness and joy,
> and sorrow and sighing shall flee away."
> Isaiah 35:10

~8~
Awake, O Sleeper

March 6, 2018

Dear friend,

There are some days that are so peaceful and my mind is so clear and still. What a gift! On those days I feel God has opened the eyes of my heart wide and I can see the world and my kids and everything in our day as it really is: in the special, God-gleaming, supernatural way. I glimpse His hand at work; the result of His work in our life and in the world seems so apparent. Those days are a joyful, needed taste of the refreshment of the soul that only comes from God. "Oh, taste and see that the Lord is good! Blessed is the man who takes refuge in him!" (Psalm 34:8).

The way I feel when I sense God at work is similar to how I feel when I stand feet planted firmly in a surprisingly warm, inviting, bright yellow patch of sunshine after a cold, dark winter day. It is as if He has awakened me to Him! It is as if He has peeled back a layer of clouds or fog that had shielded my view of His magnificent presence here with us at all times. I become awake to Him (Ephesians 5:14).

God has "woken me up" recently to notice particular moments with my children that shine His radiance and are so clearly full of Him. I could easily miss them. God is tremendously kind and tender to give us this special way of seeing Him present and active with us in our daily life as mothers. His Word is so accurate: "He will tend his flock like a shepherd; he will gather the lambs in his arms; he will carry them in his bosom, and gently lead those that are with young" (Isaiah 40:11).

Recently, for example, Liza told me how excited she was to meet the babies we expected to meet that night at the service project to which we were headed. Her heartfelt excitement reflected the wholehearted pleasure God takes in us. That joy is God-given and He is the source of it (Zephaniah 3:17).

Equally shimmering with God's radiant light was the peace and joy that Liza and one of those babies shared that night while holding hands. It reminded me of the joy we experience when we spend time with God and of His absolute enjoyment of us. Only God gives joy and peace that sweet: "You shall go out in joy and be led forth in peace... and it shall make a name for the Lord, an everlasting sign that shall not be cut off." (Isaiah 55:12a and 13b).

My oldest, Van, recently kissed me carefully and squarely on the nose, full of the kind of wholehearted sweetness that only a 5-year-old boy can share. In his kiss, I saw God's intentionality with us. I saw His individualized, personal affection for us. God tells us to "fear not, for I have redeemed you; I have called you by name, you are mine" (Isaiah 43:1b).

These remarkable little everyday moments are evidence to me, as plain as day, of God's radiance here and now, a glimpse of what is to come in His consummate fullness one glorious day when Christ returns. Truly "the path of the righteous is like the light of dawn, which shines brighter and brighter until full day" (Proverbs 4:18).

With love,
Lauren

> *"Awake, O sleeper, and arise from the dead, and Christ will shine on you."*
> *Ephesians 5:14*

✝

Lord,

I am confident and excited to anchor my soul in the firm expectation that one day when Jesus comes again to earth and You create a new heaven and a new earth, Your goodness and radiance will gleam without end. All of life's circumstances will shine Your light and point to You. All of life will cause us to say and to call out with everything in us, "Lord, I love you and you are my all!" And when I think of that, I think, "Well, let's start that all-out, full worship now!". Why wait until some later time to begin worshipping and enjoying You all the time, when You are already evident and present with us right here and right now?

Lord, awaken me regularly, please, to see with full-hearted hope the radiance of You that is all around me all the time! And to live out of that. I don't want the ease of a situation or my children's behavior to determine my gladness. My gladness (thank You and please, Lord!) comes from enjoying a close daily walk with You, my immovable Truth.

Amen.

Responding:

Day 1

Read and write Ephesians 5:14. What does it mean to you to "awake" and "arise from the dead", in a spiritual sense?

_____
_____
_____
_____

Can you think of a specific special moment you noticed recently that really illuminated God's goodness and made you feel awake to Him? Record it here. What does that moment tell you about God?

_____
_____
_____
_____

Read Isaiah 60:1-2 and write verse 2. In what ways or areas of your life have you sensed God moving you out of darkness and into His light?

_____
_____
_____
_____

Pray: Read over what you have written down in response to today's questions. Close your eyes now and talk honestly with God about what you have written and about what you are thinking and feeling.

Day 2

Read Isaiah 40:9-11 and write verse 11. In His power and kindness, God leads His people. In what specific ways has Jesus been shepherding you as you care for your young children?

_____
_____
_____
_____

Read John 1:4-5 and write verse 4 here. In what ways is Jesus your "light" in motherhood?

_____
_____
_____
_____

Read Revelation 4:8-11 and write verse 8. One day we will never stop praising God and saying how holy He is. What is one particular way you will use your life today to worship God?

_____
_____
_____
_____

Pray: Read over what you have written down in response to today's questions. Close your eyes now and talk honestly with God about what you have written and about what you are thinking and feeling.

> "Arise, shine, for your light has come,
> and the glory of the Lord has risen upon you."
> Isaiah 60:1

~9~
Praise

March 18, 2018

Dear friend,

God is showing me that singing songs of worship helps me persevere in difficult mothering moments. As I sing a song professing faith in Jesus, He calls me up to obedience in moments of weakness. When I feel like losing my temper, a song can quickly remind me to obey and honor Jesus.

God started to show me this by recently opening my mouth to sing a praise song in the middle of a hard moment with one of my kids. I was surprised to find that praising Him out loud with a song gave me a sort of road to travel. I could address the challenge His way! The song quieted my disruptive emotions and helped me to get into line behind Him. I was able to keep on singing for as long as the tricky moment required my persistence. It was a practical tool that helped me to "lay aside every weight, and sin which clings so closely, and... run with endurance the race that is set before [me], looking to Jesus, the founder and perfecter of [my] faith" (12:1-2).

I am finding that a couple of songs in particular work well for me in the tough moments that I need redirection. Singing along with "The Way (New Horizon)", I declare "Oh and I believe You are the way, the truth, the life. I believe You are" (Housefires 2018). The lyrics encourage me to live out my belief! Recalling "Spirit of God", I sing "Spirit of God, breathe on me now. Source of life, come, revive my weary heart. Spirit of God, shine on me now. Light of life, come, ignite my longing heart" (Sovereign Grace Music 2015).

Professing my faith and speaking to God in praising song prompts me to act on my faith in a way that is congruent with what I believe. Let me give you an example: Sometimes when I am changing Joel's diaper, he unintentionally kicks me - hard! Even though I feel hurt and angry, I want to give Joel Jesus instead of my frustration. So I sing at that moment, reminding myself with strenuous effort that it is Christ who returns righteousness into that challenging moment. I believe that Jesus is the only way, that He is the singular truth, and that He is the giver of all spiritual life that I require in those everyday moments (John 14:6). As I sing, I am trying to let Jesus stand there with Joel in my place, bringing love and kindness I can't muster on my own.

Believing Jesus is there working through me, I can redirect Joel in that moment, teaching him with patience and not anger. I can give him Jesus right in that upsetting mothering moment. Praising God, I restrain my sinful tendencies, and in their place, Jesus steps in. He silences my fallen nature and He provides His righteousness instead (Isaiah 45:24). What a divine exchange! The light overcomes the darkness (John 1:5). Jesus shares His ways with me (Psalm 34:9-10).

How will God use your praise of Him to cause you to follow Him closely?

With love,
Lauren

> *"For with the heart one believes and is justified, and with the mouth one confesses and is saved."*
> *Romans 10:10*

✝

Lord,

I thank You for being aware of the little moments when I need You, for being aware of my weakness and for showing up exactly when I need You. I thank You that each time I turn to You, You are completely sufficient. In Exodus 14:14, You tell us that "The Lord will fight for [us], and [we] have only to be silent", and I find that to be perfectly true. I find that as I take Your hand and choose to go Your way, it is You who enters in and rescues that moment and redeems it. I thank You that You are that powerful and that kind.

Lord, thank You for the musicians whom You have equipped to create such songs of praise that they are powerful tools for us to obey You and walk closely with You. Would You continue to inspire them to create according to Your Word? Would You use Your Word more in that powerful way? Thank You that as we open our mouths in praise of You, You grow our faith!

Lord, Your divine presence in my life is a miracle and I do not take You for granted. In my moments of strength, Your life alive in me is the reason I am able. But in the moments I am struggling, You also show Yourself present and at the ready to supply me. You are always my source, when I am high and when I am low. Would you please cause me to be so aware of Your singular sufficiency that I regularly quiet myself and choose Your way? I want that.

Amen.

Responding:

Day 1

Do you experience conflict between your emotions and your convictions in the middle of a challenging mothering moment? Think of a recent moment with your kids when you became upset. Make two lists below: on one, list the emotions you *felt* bubble to the surface; on the other, list how you *wanted* to think and act.

_____

_____

_____

_____

We have the option of exchanging our reaction for God's perspective. Read Exodus 14:13-14 and write down verse 14. How would your thoughts or behavior look differently if you were to "silence" the emotions you listed above, and instead "let the Lord fight for you"? Pray for the ability to be silent in the hard moments.

_____

_____

_____

_____

Is there a Christian worship song that you could sing in your challenging mothering moments, to keep yourself on track? Take a minute to think of a song you already know or to search online for one that speaks to you. If you need ideas, you could look up songs by Housefires, Bethel Music, or Hillsong Worship. Once you have found a song that resonates with you, allow yourself a few minutes to sit in silence and listen to it from start to finish. Make note of the song and band name here so that you can remember it and use it when you need it.

_____

_____

_____

_____

Pray: Read over what you have written down in response to today's questions. Close your eyes now and talk honestly with God about what you have written and about what you are thinking and feeling.

Day 2
Read Psalm 101:1-4 and write verse 1. Is there a time of day that you could consider regularly setting aside five minutes for listening attentively to Christian worship music, free of any distractions? How do you expect that consuming worship music and praising God as you sing along could change some of your thoughts or actions?

_____
_____
_____
_____

Read and write Proverbs 29:11. What is an area you want God to help you hold back? Is it harsh words you speak when you become upset? Is it dishonoring facial expressions? Is it a hand that is too quick to spank? Talk to God about it and ask for His active help to bring that area into submission to Him.

_____
_____
_____
_____

Read Isaiah 12:2-6 and write verse 6. Think about in what ways God has recently been "great in your midst". Make note here of a moment when He recently helped you in a specific way. Now give "praises to the Lord, for he has done gloriously" (verse 5).

_____
_____
_____

Pray: Read over what you have written down in response to today's questions. Close your eyes now and talk honestly with God about what you have written and about what you are thinking and feeling.

> *"The Lord will fight for you, and you have only to be silent."*
> *Exodus 14:14*

~10~
It Is a Good Day

April 9, 2018

Dear friend,

Yesterday God gave me a strong and sweet pep in my step as I got myself ready in the morning, a time when I am often rehearsing all the steps I can take and will have to take to make the day "good" or enjoyable. I can sometimes feel weighed down by all that the day may hold, even before the first words of the day, before I'm out of my bedroom, even my bathroom!

In the weeks prior, I had been exhausting myself, going in circles, day after day trying to manage my kids and their behavior in such a way that our day would stay smooth. But of course, no day in a house full of young children is perfectly smooth. I had been suiting up in my own strength and finding that it proved less than what I needed.

Yesterday I discovered that God had been reading my mind over those weeks. He knew I was in a state of exhaustion. He knew I had been striving for a "good" day and that I was repeatedly finding each day less than satisfactory. As my kids struggled through the same challenges as ever, as I wrestled with overcoming frustration towards them, as I repeated lessons already taught, I felt we weren't making steady progress. Any two steps forward that we took were always met by one step back, and it never felt like enough to me.

As I brushed my hair in front of the mirror yesterday, God entered in by giving me a surprising thought that was not my own. It was as if He said to me: "It *is* a good day! Every day!" I took a sharp breath in, it so surprised me to hear Him respond to my rambling, fretting thoughts. He was telling me that that day was resolutely good because we are His and because He is ours and because nothing can change that - no disappointment, no circumstance, no emotional mistake on my part, nothing. Period. The day, He was suggesting, is not to be deemed "good" at the end of the day as I breathe a sigh of relief that we got through it alright. It shouldn't be deemed "good" at the end of the day because I did a "good" job, either. Every day is good all throughout the day, from start to finish and everything in between, because it is Mine, He said, and because I Am.

As I've let this new thought from God simmer - it occurs to me that there are a few special people I know who truly live like it is a good day, no matter what the day holds. They are in agreement with God about it. They are glad for everything that comes their way because this is the day that God has made (Psalm 118:24). One of these special people I know, who trusts that the day is good because of God, will oftentimes respond with a simple "gladly!" when I've asked her for advice, or for babysitting, or for anything else. One word of joy! And with a genuine smile, too. God is most certainly the reason for her joy and for her willingness to embrace anything the day brings. She sees God at work in all things and knows that everything He is up to is great.

Could I think the same way? "Great! It's time to make dinner!" "Great! It's time to pick up the toys!" "Great! It's chores time and work is so good!" "Great! It's naptime and we are so tired." Could I learn to apply that sentiment to all of my moments, I wonder?

In the wake of this new thought, I am asking the Lord to keep on transforming and renewing my mind to think along His lines (Romans 12:2). He is literally equipping me to see and to embrace what is good and acceptable for today for my family (Romans 12:2)! He causes me to apply His truth to my everyday mothering moments. He gives me "the garment of praise instead of a faint spirit" (Isaiah 61:3). He replaces the ashes of my former way of thinking with a beautiful headdress, and He exchanges my downcast spirit with His oil of gladness (Isaiah 61:3). Jesus is my good news.

With love,
Lauren

> "This is the day that the Lord has made;
> we will rejoice and be glad in it."
> Psalm 118:24

✝

Lord,

You tell me to smile and to literally say "Great! Alright!" to the next challenging task or tantrum or moment derailing in front of me. Not cynically, but genuinely and expectantly. Because You are who You say You are, because I am Yours and You are mine and no challenge can disrupt that truth. My joining you with a pure, eyes-on-You attitude of joy and expectation in what You are up to gives You all the more opportunity to show Yourself strong and gentle and true.

You replace my feeble mindset with Your unchanging truth. Thank You for the special moments by which You enter my days and rescue me from approaching them from any perspective other than Yours. May I apply Your instruction now, by Your strength, to all of my good days. Be glorified, Lord, in all that You are up to in my family.

Amen.

Responding:

Day 1

Complete the below chart to answer these questions: What tend to be your first thoughts each morning? How do you think God wants to transform your natural way of thinking to match His own?

Your natural first thoughts:	How God wants to transform those thoughts:

Read and write Psalm 118:24. On what basis do you typically judge how "good" a day has been? Is it based on how well you have managed it, how others have behaved in it, or what you have accomplished in it? If so, confess that to God and ask Him to help you see each day as good simply because it is His.

_____
_____
_____
_____

Choose a moment you expect to arise later on today that is often challenging for you. If you decide that today's being a "good" day does not depend on the outcome of that circumstance, how would you approach the situation differently? When that situation arises later, plan to say "Great! Alright!" and embrace it as part of the good day God has made.

_____
_____
_____

Pray: Read over what you have written down in response to today's questions. Close your eyes now and talk honestly with God about what you have written and about what you are thinking and feeling.

Day 2

How did it go yesterday when you said "Great!" to God's good day during a challenging moment? Did you have a smidge more gentleness, kindness, or clarity of mind than you usually do in that situation? Did anything else notable result from your taking God's perspective on the situation?

_____
_____
_____
_____

Read Psalm 5:11-12 and write verse 11. Look up the definition for the word "exult". What connection do you see between joy and walking closely with God?

_____
_____
_____
_____

Read Romans 12:1-2 in The Message translation. What part of your day today would it be new for you to "place before God as an offering"?

_____
_____
_____

Pray: Read over what you have written down in response to today's questions. Close your eyes now and talk honestly with God about what you have written and about what you are thinking and feeling.

"Let me hear what God the Lord will speak, for he will speak peace to his people, to his saints; but let them not turn back to folly. Surely his salvation is near to those who fear him, that glory may dwell in our land."

Psalm 85:8-9

Reflection

Take a few minutes to look back through the notes you've made on the responding questions for entries 1 through 10.

❀ What recurring topics and themes do you see showing up?

_____
_____
_____
_____

❀ What stands out to you about those recurring topics?

_____
_____
_____
_____

❀ What do you sense God nudging you to know about Him or about your relationship with Him?

_____
_____
_____
_____

❀ How do you think God wants you to apply what He is telling you?

_____
_____
_____
_____

❁ Tell God what questions you have for Him. Make a note of them here so that you remember what you asked Him and can watch for His direction in response.

_____
_____
_____
_____

❁ Thank God for being very present with you and entering into the details of your everyday life with you.

_____
_____
_____
_____

~11~
Abundance

April 20, 2018

Dear friend,

At the start of my kids' naptime one day recently, God gently sat me down at my kitchen table with a spiral notebook and pen, and He had me hash out how I would spend the time that I have each day during my kids' naptime. I knew He wanted me to do it because I sensed that the direction I would receive from Him would bless my doing (James 1:25). Over the years, God and I have hashed out this plan several times. As my family's routines change to allow for new naptimes or preschool or other schedule shifts, I have revisited my daily quiet time plan to accommodate those changes.

That afternoon I wrote out the following plan for my daily naptime window:

2:15-2:30 PM: Start a load of laundry / Tidy up from the morning
2:30-3:00 PM: Bible study
3:00-3:15 PM: Prayer time
3:15-3:30 PM: Prep after-nap snack / List kids' afternoon chores
3:30-4:00 PM: Prep dinner to get a jump start on it before the kids are awake

For me, creating a plan for how to use my daily quiet time is not about getting a rush from checking things off of a list. Instead, it has to do with aligning my path with God's priorities. When I follow God's direction on how I spend my time, it is like He has provided me with a railroad track to follow. On days when I tend toward indecision, I no longer hem and haw over what to do first and next or whether I've prioritized what I should. His plan serves as my guide to keep me or put me back on His purposeful track.

Without God's plan, I can tend to forget where I find the refreshment I need to walk closely with Him through the second half of the day once everyone is awake again and in need. When I follow His priorities, making the most of my quiet time doesn't depend on how our day has gone or what my present perspective is; rather, I know Who remains in charge regardless, and I know what He's said to do. My eyes stay focused on Him. It is so freeing to me to operate in God's plan and not out of my own fluctuating emotions.

Having jotted down my updated quiet time plan that day, I was surprised to find that it wasn't quite 2:30pm yet and I felt I had a few free minutes. I checked my email inbox. I found an email from a friend from church. He had sent a group of us a link to an article by a popular author on parenting (Rosemond 2018). Our friend said how useful the author's guidance had been to him and his wife. I clicked the link, and its contents landed like a big surprise gift smack in the middle of our kitchen table.

God used that friend's email and the author's wisdom to equip me in parenting in a new way that day. The thrust of the article was that if we as parents are to have authority over our children, we must exercise it. We must not only see ourselves as the authority but we must behave as the active authority in our children's lives. If, for example, I have set an expectation or I give an instruction to my children, and they do not meet it, I must uphold my expectation and so uphold the value of my authority in their lives. To allow my children to disregard an instruction - without consequence - undermines my authority and forfeits its value. If I do not implement my authority, I effectively have none.

Using that article, God showed me in a fresh way that I hadn't yet internalized the fact that using my authority is part and parcel of loving my children. While He wants me to be loving and forgiving towards my children as they learn and grow, the grace I show them must not be to the detriment of my authority to guide them into godly living. I cannot expect to show them grace alone - generosity of spirit when it is undeserved. My love towards them must also involve firm expectations that they live according to the plans God has laid out for us. In other words, the grace I show them has to be paired with truth (John 1:14). And so my following through on what I've said they must do or what I've said I will do is essential to living according to His divine design. I am not raising my children to serve themselves; I am raising them to serve the one true living God, whose authority over them is present and eternal. That will unequivocally require me to call them up to a higher standard and exercise my God-given authority (Ephesians 4:1).

As I parent my young children, exercising my authority requires that I hold the line and impose consequences that will make an impression on my children. Doing that feels uncomfortable! The part of me that leans on my own understanding instead of God's wisdom (Proverbs 3:5-6) fears that holding the line and imposing consequences comes off as too harsh. I fear my children will think my expectations are requiring perfection of them.

But God has shown me that exercising my authority is not inherently harsh - it is an essential part of loving my children into learning how to live His way. There will be many times that I will have to put my foot down firmly in order to be effective in calling them up into godly behavior. Just like I require His guidance, they too need to know where His track is.

Proverbs 19:21 says that "many are the plans in the mind of a man, but it is the purpose of the Lord that will stand". The afternoon that God sat me down at my kitchen table recently served a far grander purpose than I had realized it would. God ordered my plans that day and then also solidified His purpose in them. He met me in my meager faithfulness in order to share His exceedingly abundant wisdom and goodness with me! God is "able to do far more abundantly than all that we ask or think" (Ephesians 3:20). You and I are the thankful recipients of God's abiding instruction and love.

With love,
Lauren

> "Many are the plans in the mind of a man, but it is the purpose of the Lord that will stand."
> Proverbs 19:21

†

Lord,

You are so generous with how You help me. You sat me down that day to help me stay on track during my quiet times, so that I could carry on in Your strength through the second half of my days. You met me in the nitty-gritty of life and showed me that no detail is too small for You. You set my course.

I thank You that You outdid Yourself that day in not only setting my course but in giving me a fresh wind in my sails, too. You used that friend's email and the surprise article to remove a veil from my eyes that I hadn't realized had been there. I hadn't realized I needed a fresh "okay" from you to carry on and do what You have called me to do. Thank You for reminding me that my loving, shepherding authority over my children is for their good even when it is uncomfortable for me. That reminds me not only to pray that they submit to You but also to require it of them myself. That is a fine distinction and You knew I needed You to point it out. Thank You that You did! You equip me in more ways than I know to ask. You are generous with Your love in action towards me.

Amen.

Responding:

Day 1

What is your comfort level with your role as an authority over your children? How does understanding that God is your own authority impact your comfort level with exercising your authority over your children?

_____
_____
_____
_____

Are you ever afraid that your children will perceive you as unloving if you uphold your expectations or impose consequences upon them? Read Psalm 32:10 and write it down here. With what does God promise to surround those who trust in Him?

_____
_____
_____
_____

Read Psalm 32:8-11 and write verse 8. What instruction has God been giving you lately? How does it make you feel to know that He is guiding you and helping you along?

_____
_____
_____
_____

Pray: Read over what you have written down in response to today's questions. Close your eyes now and talk honestly with God about what you have written and about what you are thinking and feeling.

Day 2

What could be your regular "quiet time" routine so that you find refreshment from God for the rest of the day? What will be your daily plan to spend time reading His Word and praying?

_____
_____
_____
_____

Read and write Ephesians 3:20. How has God recently dealt with you "abundantly"? List three ways, even if you have to think hard to come up with them all.

_____
_____
_____
_____

Look back to Ephesians 3:20 from the previous question. In what way do you think your reliance on Jesus in the everyday moments is impacting the next generation in your family?

_____
_____
_____

Pray: Read over what you have written down in response to today's questions. Close your eyes now and talk honestly with God about what you have written and about what you are thinking and feeling.

> "To Him who is able to do far more abundantly than all we ask or think, according to the power at work within us, to him be glory in the church and in Christ Jesus throughout all generations, forever and ever. Amen."
> Ephesians 3:20

~12~
Blessed Work

May 19, 2018

Dear friend,

There are so many little tasks involved in being a mother. I tend to be a worker; it's the way God made me. And so I enjoy most of the recurring details and tasks that are my responsibility each day. Cooking, meal planning, laundry, managing school papers that come home, and so on. I enjoy much of that work because I really like bringing order to things and because I find it enjoyable to have variety in my days.

But at the same time, I have always struggled as a mom with guilt over enjoying those tasks. I have felt like I should want to be fully present and engaged with my kids throughout the day. I have felt guilty that I sometimes would rather get some of my work done than engage with my children. I have struggled with how to set aside time during the day to finish the work I need to, while feeling comfortable with what they are doing while I work. At first, when I had only one child, my concern was that I was ignoring him. As our family grew to having two children and now three, I have often had that same lingering guilt, but now it is compounded by the additional challenge of wanting my kids to be peaceful and to get along with each other while I am attending to other things.

Beyond those child-related concerns, I have also struggled to think about work and play in a healthy way. I have felt that if I was working and really enjoying it, I must not be working hard enough. Play time or free time, on the other hand, has often felt to me like getting away with something.

But God has shown me that all of those ways of thinking are erroneous. It is a gift from God that working hard can be thoroughly enjoyable. Enjoying my work is an expression of my faithfulness to Him and the responsibilities He has given me (Psalm 37:3). Playing, relaxing, and even sleeping enough are deeply important and worthy of my time (Psalm 127:2). They are not playing hooky from what "really matters" in life. I am rightly free to enjoy the variety of elements God has chosen to make part of my days.

As I ask God for guidance in these things that are hard for me to sort out, God is maturing me and bringing me emotional freedom. For one thing, God is reminding me that He made me exactly as I am. Each part of me is intended to bring Him glory, whether I am cleaning or organizing or helping my children or playing with them (1 Corinthians 10:31). Following Him, I get to feel settled about the various parts of my days and investing time into them.

Secondly, it's His plan that I actually enjoy the work that He has given me to do. I can and I should embrace it. When I'm living according to His design, I get to feel satisfied (Proverbs 19:23)! My joy in accomplishing the work He's given me is part of His plan in the first place. I need not - in fact, must not - grieve Him by waffling over the joy of working for Him. His Word instructs me that whatever I do, I should do heartily, as for Him (Colossians 3:23)!

Additionally, when I work gladly, instead of worrying about it, I am free to be genuinely present and kind towards my children when we are spending time together.

The freedom God is bringing me around the topic of work is allowing me to do more work when my kids are awake, which is new for me. I don't have to squeeze all my laundering, dishwashing, vacuuming, or other chores into their naptimes or after their bedtime. With them around while I work, I can even model for them the blessing of enjoying work.

God has allowed me most recently to discover that I enjoy weeding our garden beds. While I weed and my kids be-bop around in the backyard without my management, that task has become a special shared interest with my youngest child, Joel. As I weed, he and I find worms - a real treasure for him. That particular part of my work has become playful. What a new discovery for me! In those kinds of moments, God is showing me that work and play need not be completely separate from one another. Infused with His glorious perspective, my work now feels blessed to me, and I see that it has been all along.

With love,
Lauren

> "Trust in the Lord and do good;
> dwell in the land and befriend faithfulness."
> Psalm 37:3

✝ *Lord,*

Thank You for the freedom that You grant me to enjoy all of the parts of my life that You have so graciously given to me. Thank You that You free me from wrong patterns of thinking, and that You replace my wrong thinking with changes in perspective that bring the peace and joy that are evidence of You and Your participation in my life. Would you please calm my heart throughout my days so that I hear You and say "yes" to You? I want to enter into the glory You have planned for each part of my day. I know that there is work that You have assigned me to do and I now see that I am free to enjoy it. You give me eyes to see Your glory, Your goodness, in each part of my life and my family's life.

Thank You, Lord, for patiently guiding me through these complexities of life as a mother!

Amen.

Responding:

Day 1

Read Genesis 1:26-2:3 and 2:15 and notice that when God first made man and put him in the Garden of Eden, He gave him abundant work to do. Write Genesis 2:15 here. How does it make you feel that God has work for you to do?

_____
_____
_____
_____

We have looked at Romans 11:36 previously in our study and we return to it today. Read and write that verse here. Do you tend to struggle more with embracing work or free time, and why? How does your thinking about that area of your life change when you perceive that there is glory for God in it?

_____
_____
_____
_____

God's Word promises that we find life, joy, and pleasure in living the way He has designed. Read Psalm 16:1-11 and write verse 11. In what ways will freely welcoming all of the different parts of your life bring more joy into your days?

_____
_____
_____
_____

Pray: Read over what you have written down in response to today's questions. Close your eyes now and talk honestly with God about what you have written and about what you are thinking and feeling.

Day 2

Read and write Psalm 37:3. God commands us to trust Him. What wrong patterns of thinking about your work and your responsibilities will you turn over to Him?

_____
_____
_____
_____

Read Proverbs 3:5-8 and write verse 5. Pray that God will show you any errors in your accepted ways of doing things.

_____
_____
_____
_____

Read Psalm 86:1-12 and write verse 11. What area of your heart is still "divided" in terms of trusting God? Write it down here and then pray this verse back to God, asking Him to unite your heart to submit completely to Him.

_____
_____
_____
_____

Pray: Read over what you have written down in response to today's questions. Close your eyes now and talk honestly with God about what you have written and about what you are thinking and feeling.

"Teach me your way, O Lord,
that I may walk in your truth;
unite my heart to fear your name."
Psalm 86:11

~13~
Burdened

June 14, 2018

Dear friend,

At times, I become overwhelmed with the expectations I have set up for myself as a mom. I start thinking I need a chart for this certain problem behavior and a chart for that, and how have I possibly overlooked "x" and not noticed we need that, too?!

At those times my mind becomes bogged down and cluttered and I am so stuck in the circumstances right in front of me. Doing mothering right becomes an overwhelming burden.

The other day my wise and well-spoken husband reminded me as I nervously voiced those anxieties to him that "His burden is light":

**"Come to me, all who labor and are heavy laden, and I will give you rest.
Take my yoke upon you, and learn from me,
for I am gentle and lowly in heart,
and you will find rest for your souls.
For my yoke is easy,
and my burden is light."
Matthew 11:28-30**

When my husband reminded me that Jesus' burden is light, I appreciated his compassion and wisdom, but the message didn't immediately hit home in my heart. Later on that night, exasperated at the end of a taxing day, I needed a change of pace. I got onto my treadmill and vented to God in prayer. It was an emotional prayer. I poured out my burdened mind and my overwhelmed soul. I did not sugar-coat it!

"But God, being rich in mercy, because of the great love with which he loved us, even when we were dead in our trespasses, made us alive together with Christ" (Ephesians 2:4-5).

Suddenly, in the midst of that run, I remembered my husband's words and I smiled: "His burden is light". God used those four specific words from His living Word and my loving husband's kindness to provide Himself to me in a deeply spiritual way in that moment during my run. By bringing that phrase to my mind in that very burdened moment, in response to my crying out to Him, God reached in and plucked away that overbearing sense I had had of my insufficiency and the magnitude of how much "getting it right" mattered. As soon as He did it, that burden was simply and beautifully gone. That smile came across my face because in place of the burden, God gave me full-hearted, peace-filled certainty that the work happening in my children's hearts is actually *His* own work. The burden is *His* to carry.

God showed me in that moment on the treadmill that He is the One acting in my family. He is the One at work from a much wider perspective. While He has me doing important work in support of His great work, His grand plan of imprinting Himself on my children's hearts is so much deeper, so much more soul-satisfying, and far more God-glorifying than any good effort I can concoct on my own. The most valuable contribution that I make to raising my children, He showed me, is quieting down and letting Him use me as His vessel (2 Corinthians 4:7). Even the valuable work that I do is still His work.

In my utter weakness and insufficiency, at the end of my rope, God met me exactly where I was. His righteous, bright light shone on me in the middle of that run, when it was late, when I was sweaty and upset, and when I least anticipated it. God met me in that unexpected moment and redefined the mothering road ahead of me. Receiving His peace that night was like feeling a gentle wave of His love sweeping over me. I came to Him with a slew of emotional questions about what to do next and how to muster up the ability in me to do any of it. He replied as if by lovingly whispering, "You're asking the wrong question. You're not the answer. I Am."

While sometimes God spells out the details for me, in this instance, God comforted me with a deep reminder of His authority and His responsibility over my children (Psalm 46:10). He quieted me with His love (Zephaniah 3:17). He showed up in His power and supremacy and reminded me of my humble place in His great big, eternal Kingdom, reorienting my perspective to Him. He led me to the foot of His throne, before His awesome and holy and faithful Self. His active presence with me is "the goodness of the Lord in the land of the living" (Psalm 27:13).

With love,
Lauren

> *"The Lord Your God is in your midst,*
> *a mighty one who will save;*
> *he will rejoice over you with gladness;*
> *he will quiet you by his love;*
> *he will exult over you with loud singing."*
> *Zephaniah 3:17*

✝

Lord,

Each and every day You speak to my children's hearts and call them by name, drawing them to You in Your personal way. You ignite, stoke, and nurture the changes You bring about in their character, transforming their hearts little by little as You mold them. I believe - because You say You are - that You are transforming their hearts, like You are my own, by one degree of glory to another (2 Corinthians 3:18). I believe You are teaching my children to live in a way that reflects the changes You bring about in their hearts and minds. I believe You will cause them to love to live for You. It is You who gives them both the will and the way to live for You and with You.

Give me grace, Lord, to mother them in a way that lives out my trust in Your authority over their lives and Your loving shepherding of them. I wish I could be as steady as You are, but I so often fall short as I care for them. I get so upset when their behavior is repeatedly contrary to my instruction and Yours. I want them to see and to know without a doubt that being a new creation in You matters, that following You changes us and our perspective on everything. I want to follow You closely, and I want them to do the same. Transform me, Lord, I ask, so that I can point them to life in You.

Thank You, Lord, that by Your love, strength, and sovereignty, You are at work in my children's hearts. I trust that You alone are the mighty One who will save (Zephaniah 3:17).

Amen.

Responding:

Day 1

With what are you heavy laden in this season of parenting? Write your thoughts below. Then read and write Matthew 11:28. Hear the Lord inviting you to come to Him with that specific burden and to leave that burden with Him. Take the time to do that right now.

_____
_____
_____
_____

Which of your responsibilities for your children do you fear you will not do "successfully" for them? List those concerns here specifically.

_____
_____
_____
_____

What are you afraid will happen if you don't mother your children the way you envision? List your fears and imagine laying each one down at the foot of the cross. Then read and write Psalm 34:4.

_____
_____
_____
_____

Pray: Read over what you have written down in response to today's questions. Close your eyes now and talk honestly with God about what you have written and about what you are thinking and feeling.

Day 2

Read Matthew 11:29-30 and write verse 29 here. A yoke is a wooden crosspiece fastened over the necks of two animals and attached to the load they are to pull together. What does it mean to you to take Jesus' yoke upon you?

___

In Matthew 11:29 Jesus says he is "gentle and lowly in heart". How would following His example of being gentle and lowly in heart in the midst of your parenting trials change your outlook and behavior?

___

God rescues our burdened souls now during our earthly life as a foretaste of the abiding rest we will have in heaven with Him for eternity. Read and write Zephaniah 3:17. Which element of this truth do you need to fully receive into your heart today?

___

Pray: Read over what you have written down in response to today's questions. Close your eyes now and talk honestly with God about what you have written and about what you are thinking and feeling.

"I sought the Lord, and he answered me and delivered me from all my fears."
Psalm 34:4

~14~
He Will Establish Your Plans

June 20, 2018

Dear friend,

The summer began last week and it felt like it was stretching out endlessly in front of me. Lacking our usual school schedule, I felt a little at loose ends. Also, my husband and I had been trying to find the most effective way to instill first-time obedience in our kids. Because I wasn't yet sure enough of our new summer routine, I didn't know what I wanted to expect of my kids in terms of their behavior at various times of the day. They must have sensed my indecision, because they were pushing the envelope and testing the limits. One morning, in a quiet moment on my own, I cried over it, and all I could get out to say to God was: "God, I just need you to give me some ideas." I left it at that because I didn't know how else to pray about it; I had reached the end of my understanding and my creativity. I knew His wisdom would satisfy the situation, at least in time, and I was eager for it to come soon. I was inclining my ear and in need of Him to come to me (Isaiah 55:3).

God answered my direct prayer quickly and concretely (Psalm 34:4). That very morning, He gave me a specific way to clarify for my kids and for myself my expectations of them in each part of the day. He simply gave me the idea, as if He dropped it right out of the sky and into my brain. It was another thought that wasn't mine; it was His: He told me to post a visible schedule for our days, to outline what would be happening during each part of the day. How straightforward! It was such a relief to me to know what to do next.

I set to work that afternoon because I knew I was following His lead. I am so thankful He had me believe that it was Him leading me to create the schedule from the get-go. I could really sink my teeth into it because it was the help I had asked for (Isaiah 55:2-3).

What I wrote down as our schedule is nearly what we naturally did already, but writing it down made our daily plans and my expectations during each part of the day clear for us all (see Appendix 1 for the schedule itself). I felt authorized to go ahead and carry out each part of our days. It also allowed me to be certain that I have in fact been clear to my children about my expectations of them.

Now, equipped with God's idea, following His lead, I am feeling confident about giving my kids scheduled, alone free time between 9 and 10 a.m. each morning.

Time after breakfast had always been unplanned. Our new, written, posted schedule has given me God's awesome authorization to be completely present wherever I need to be during that hour of the day. That is new to me! Suddenly, my mind does not need to try to be in several places at once. I can be focused and satisfied while cleaning up from breakfast, putting in some laundry, dressing Joel, starting something in the crockpot, or making a brief phone call.

For our afternoon time, I felt I had received God's "okay" to send my older two out into the backyard after afternoon snack, without me. I am feeling like I can do that cheerfully, leading them to embrace some imaginative, active playtime together instead of fretting it will be repetitive day after day. That allows me to embrace a peaceful time cooking dinner while Joel plays in the family room.

I am seeing - all of a sudden and all throughout the day - that I don't have to run ragged and feel stretched thin in too many directions, trying to meet everyone's needs all at once. God's intention for me as a mother is not to meet everyone's myriad needs all at once. He is the only One who can truly satisfy us! I need not attempt to take on that impossible task. And nothing will be impossible for Him (Luke 1:37).

As I have begun to put His idea for a clear plan for our days into action, God has also whispered to my heart that we are to consecrate, or set apart, each part of the day to Him. Each part of the day is His. At once both righteous and loving, He has instructed me not to diminish His glory by worrying about whether a certain part of the day is "enough". He has set my schedule for me and He has shown me that there is glory and worship and praise for Him to receive in each and every last part of it. He is teaching me to commit all that I do to Him, and as He promises, He is so very personally establishing even my routine, everyday plans (Proverbs 16:3).

With love,
Lauren

> *"Give ear, O Lord, to my prayer;*
> *listen to my plea for grace.*
> *In the day of my trouble I call upon you,*
> *for you answer me."*
> *Psalm 86:6-7*

✝

Lord,

Thank You for showing such kindness to me that You listened to my need and met me exactly there. You did not leave me to fend for myself. You answered me when I needed You. You are faithful towards me.

Thank You, Lord, that You know what is best for us, and thank You that You communicate to us how to live that out. You gently reminded me to set aside my preoccupations about how I organize our days. You gave me the beautiful freedom to wholeheartedly agree with You and Your plans for our day, and I see now that You get glory from each part of our walking closely with You. There is nothing more that I could ever want for our days than Your glory.

You wrap up my joy in Your glory. You establish my plans. Thank you for answering my blundering, desperate, heartfelt request, and in doing so, for connecting my good with Your glory.

Amen.

Responding:

Day 1

Read and write Proverbs 16:3. In what specific area of parenting are you in need of God's direction?

___

What direction do you sense God may have already given you about how to handle the area of parenting you identified in the previous question? Read and write Psalm 86:6-7 and then pray it out loud.

___

God tells us that He sees our circumstances and our needs. Read Isaiah 49:15-16 and write verse 16. How does it impact you to know that God is continually and intimately attuned to us and our "walls"?

_____
_____
_____
_____

Pray: Read over what you have written down in response to today's questions. Close your eyes now and talk honestly with God about what you have written and about what you are thinking and feeling.

Day 2
Imagine in your mind's eye that a parenting area in which you are feeling empty-handed is an empty jar. Our emptiness and awareness of our need is exactly what is needed to receive what the Lord pours into us. Read and write 2 Corinthians 12:9-10.

_____
_____
_____
_____

Read Psalm 143:8-10 and write verse 10. What connection do you see between God's love for us and His instruction to us?

_____
_____
_____
_____

Have you noticed that even the dryness we sense when we are in need shows how amazing and glorious God is? When we have really perceived the depth of our need to hear from God, and then we do hear from Him, we realize that the solution in that area did not come from ourselves, but from God! Read and write John 7:37-38.

_____
_____
_____
_____

Pray: Read over what you have written down in response to today's questions. Close your eyes now and talk honestly with God about what you have written and about what you are thinking and feeling.

> *"Commit to the Lord whatever you do, and he will establish your plans."*
> Proverbs 16:3 (NIV)

~15~
Attention

September 17, 2018

Dear friend,

There is something so undeniably important about looking each other in the eyes when we talk and when we listen to each other. I try to teach this truth to my children. "Let me see your eyes", I tell our oldest, who tends to split his attention between a couple of things at once. "Stop, look, and listen," I find myself repeating to them. When my children want my attention, I see them watching, too, to make sure my eyes are turned to them and stay there until they are finished.

While I try to teach my children to listen attentively, I find I struggle to do it myself! My attention is divided as I try to simultaneously listen to one of my children, give another a nod of encouragement, and cook dinner. I quickly become stretched too thin! My tone gets sharp, my responses are clipped, and I don't do any one of the three things well. My children don't learn well from that example, either. By addressing their needs as soon as they arise, I am not teaching them to develop patience. I don't want to continue in that pattern, but I struggle to know how to address all that I must. How do I do all of this, Lord?, I've asked Him.

God has seen me identifying these dynamics and He is responding by speaking His life into our everyday moments (Isaiah 55:2). He has recently guided me to set up several clear and loving boundaries around attention:

- I have sensed God telling me to go ahead and focus on the task at hand. "Let your eyes look directly forward, and your gaze be straight before you", as Proverbs 4:25 says. When I am making breakfast, for example, God has given me the peace I need to gently tell my kids to bring a quiet toy to the table instead of allowing them to get too busy and noisy for those early morning hours. Too much activity in the morning ends up requiring my intervention and it's not a time I'm really available for them. He gave me the sense of His "okay" to tell them to hold off on sharing their thoughts with me until we sit down at the breakfast table together instead of intermittently chatting to me while I cook. This keeps me from becoming agitated. I come to the table ready to give, instead of feeling drained before we have begun.

Once, when I felt I would burst with the frustration of their simultaneous comments, out blurted an unintentionally funny line that tickled them and surprised me. (Thank You, Holy Spirit, for Your words!) "Hold that thought like a runaway horse!", I had said with a smile. My children loved it. I still got to hold onto my making breakfast now and listening later, my sanity remained intact, and everyone felt loved. It was a special moment when God really showed Himself present in the nitty-gritty of our days. He gave me a line to say and it made us laugh! It felt as though He had rewarded me for trying to listen in the depths of my heart, even when I felt I was too weak to follow Him well myself.

- God has also quieted my mind by guiding me to limit noise in the car. I have recently set the "rule" with a gentle smile that I will be the one to choose and set the music: whether or not it's on, what we listen to, its volume. I also choose whether the windows will be up or down. The rare, polite request I allow, but in general, the car ride is at my discretion. In the car my kids are free to enjoy books, to play with a small toy, to listen to the music, or to look out the window. Eliminating requests in the car has allowed us all to relax and enjoy a peaceful ride. God's direction to us extends even to the car!

- God has also let me feel that it is okay and sometimes it is best for me to tell my children with a genuinely gentle smile that I would love for us to be in the same room together but that I cannot talk or listen right now. The opportunity for togetherness but with quiet minds steadies the flow of activity, so crucial for me as I manage our day and pay attention to God's direction. I know that a quiet mind under His direct care is a huge factor in my ability to control my tongue: the words I do say, the tone I use, and the words I do not say to my kids. Reserving mental space to pay attention to God, He shares His peace and faithfulness with me, so that I have it to give away, too (Isaiah 26:3-4).

God intends for the life He offers to trickle down into the crevices and details of our daily life as a family. His instruction is life-giving to me and to my children (John 10:10). Yet again I see that Jesus truly is the singular way, truth, and life for every nuanced aspect of our lives (John 14:6).

With love,
Lauren

"O Lord, you will ordain peace for us, for you have indeed done for us all our works."
Isaiah 26:12

†

Lord,

Thank You, Lord, that as I list out the very particular ways You have guided me, I see that You are not above the details of my life. You know the limits of my mind and the frailty of my flesh. In utterly practical ways, You show me how to build my life on You, and You are always enough. Please keep on, Lord! I need You.

Amen.

Responding:

Day 1

Read Proverbs 4:20-27 and write verse 25. In which parts of your day do you find yourself becoming frustrated or short-tempered with your kids because you are doing too much? What healthy boundary could you set around that particular time in order to remain kind?

In the previous question you identified a healthy boundary you can put in place in order to protect your attention to God and preserve your kindness towards those around you. From the Proverbs 4 verses you read, write verses 20 and 22. How do you expect that staying close to God in what have been difficult moments will actually bring healing to your flesh?

Reread Proverbs 4:20-27. Write verse 23. Name two particular upcoming parts of your day during which you will commit to "keeping your heart [under God's authority] with all vigilance".

Pray: Read over what you have written down in response to today's questions. Close your eyes now and talk honestly with God about what you have written and about what you are thinking and feeling.

Day 2

Read Ephesians 4:29-32 and write verse 32. Take a moment to consider how you speak to your children. What aspect of your speech may you need to bring further into submission to God: your words, your tone, your facial expressions, or what you leave unspoken?

Read Proverbs 13:3 and 15:1-5. Write Proverbs 15:1. Was there a moment this week that you spoke harshly to your children? Write down what you said, and then write down what or how you could speak differently the next time that same situation arises.

Read Proverbs 18:20-21 and write verse 21. What connection do you experience between reserving some mental space to listen to God and your ability to treat your children lovingly?

Pray: Read over what you have written down in response to today's questions. Close your eyes now and talk honestly with God about what you have written and about what you are thinking and feeling.

> "My son, be attentive to my words;
> incline your ear to my sayings...
> For they are life to those who find them,
> and healing to all their flesh."
> Proverbs 4:20, 22

~16~
Our Cause

November 9, 2018

Dear friend,

I have a dry erase board that sits in my kitchen bay window. The board almost always has a Bible verse on it, one that's been having a powerful impact on me recently.

Last week, my 6-year-old, Van, noticed that the dry erase board did not have anything written on it. My dry erase markers had run dry and the previous message had been smeared away by lots of little finger swipes. My son asked in a confused and mildly alarmed voice, "Why haven't you written anything on this?!"

That little moment with Van showed me that my children notice the smallest of details. I saw that the verses I put up on that board, and the life God breathes into our days through them, were paving their way into my children's young hearts. Van's question that day was a small but powerful reminder to me to keep diligently at work weaving our reliance on God and His love into the little details of our family's life. I see that God is cultivating His ways in my children's hearts because of the simple presence of His Word literally at their fingertips.

During my kids' naptime and my Bible quiet time on the day of that brief conversation with Van, I made some notes in my journal. I wrote down practical ideas about how I want to go about parenting hand in hand with God. The moment with Van had caused me to look concretely at our days to see how I could be more intentional about pointing my children to Jesus. I asked myself, How can I work along with God so that our everyday life even more richly reflects His presence? I want to be sowing deliberately into their hearts where He is already present and reaping. It was a brainstorming session and as I sat down to make note of my thoughts, I had the impression that God was ordering my thoughts. It felt like He took what had been my smattering of ideas and caused them to gel together according to His purpose. What I wrote down ended up falling into four categories:

- My goal in raising my children: What do Jeff and I seek to do?
- Strategies to align our parenting with that goal: At their young ages right now, how can we begin training our children toward that goal?

- Our mindset: What do Jeff and I want the prevailing attitudes of our family to be as we work towards that goal?
- The centrality of God's Word to our family's life: How will we weave God's Word into our daily life?

You can read my detailed notes on these topics in Appendix 2 if you wish. In short, God helped me start to align our family's goals with everyday strategies, so that we could be sure we were actively working with Him towards our goals. As our children get older and as Jeff and I learn more ourselves, the details of our parenting plan with God will take on new facets. But the list I made that day was a helpful start for us with our children's current ages. Because I sensed God organizing my thoughts, I knew He was leading me. Knowing that I am following Him is giving me such joy and certainty as I go about our everyday moments!

I was eager after that brainstorming session to begin to weave God's Word into our daily life more. I sat down with my Bible and found a dozen or so short Bible verses, and I wrote each one down on a separate card. I matched each verse to the tune of a well-known song so that we could begin to memorize them. I have begun to string the verses up together so that they are a regularly visible reminder of the impact His Word should have on our thinking and doing. In Appendix 3, you can see a photo of some of the verses hanging and a list of the tunes that are helping us memorize them. I hope you will use them and come up with others yourself, too.

I could have seen that day's brainstorming session as my own idea, but I don't believe that's what it was. I believe that it was God who opened my ears to that little comment from Van that day. It was God who spurred me on to take the impact of His presence and His Word on us further. It is He who inspires us and fills our sails with Himself, equipped for the next segment of life lived with Him. God fulfills His promise: "So shall my word be that goes out from my mouth; it shall not return to me empty, but it shall accomplish that which I purpose, and shall succeed in the thing for which I sent it." (Isaiah 55:11).

God used the fact that I had noticed my kids' responsiveness to His Word to reorient me to my *cause* in parenting. My cause, my driving goal, has been to disciple my children to follow Jesus and to see that true life is found only in Him. Indeed "may He maintain the cause of His servant as each day requires, that all the peoples may know that the Lord is God" (1 Kings 8:59-60).

In more little, everyday ways than we can imagine, God is using His Word to accomplish His purpose of aligning our hearts with Him.

With love,
Lauren

> *"May he maintain the cause of his servant as each day requires, that all the peoples may know that the Lord is God; there is no other."*
> **1 Kings 8:59-60**

†

Lord,

It is You who causes us to want to parent together with You.

It is also You who causes us to learn ways of breaking that conviction down into the stuff of everyday life. Thank You that You are a part of our lives in very personal ways.

I need You, Lord, to keep on guiding me like You are doing - causing me to see with the eyes of my heart how You want me to parent together with You and inspiring me to materialize that conviction. I need You to maintain my cause - Your glory - because You are both my will and my way (Philippians 2:13).

Please cause me to be keenly aware of Your presence and the life we find only in You. Please lead my children to know that You are truly God, that there is no other (Deuteronomy 4:35).

Amen.

Responding:

Day 1
Read and write 1 Corinthians 10:31. Have you decided to make God the cause, or goal, of your parenting? What does that mean to you?

_____
_____
_____
_____

God had me write down some specific notes about how I want to go about parenting more closely with Him (Appendix 2). How do you want to go about mothering hand in hand with God even more deliberately than you have? Make some notes about how you could weave God into your day in practical ways, and see where God leads you in your thinking.

_____

_____

_____

_____

Read 1 Kings 8:56-61. Notice how verse 59 says that "each day requires" that God lead us to keep our eyes fixed on Him. Write verse 60. What does the word "that" at the beginning of verse 60 indicate?

_____

_____

_____

_____

Pray: Read over what you have written down in response to today's questions. Close your eyes now and talk honestly with God about what you have written and about what you are thinking and feeling.

Day 2

Read and write Habakkuk 2:2. Then read your notes from yesterday about how you want to mother your children even more deliberately together with God, and see what you might add to your plan of ideas today.

_____

_____

_____

_____

Read Acts 19:20 and write it here. God's Word has a powerful impact on all who hear it. Is there a special verse you want to teach to your kids or post in your home?

_____

_____

_____

_____

Read Matthew 13:18-23 and write verse 23. Pray for each of your children by name right now, asking Him to use their hearing of His Word to cause deep-rooted faith to grow in their hearts.

_____
_____
_____
_____

Pray: Read over what you have written down in response to today's questions. Close your eyes now and talk honestly with God about what you have written and about what you are thinking and feeling.

> "For it is God who works in you,
> both to will and to work for his good pleasure."
> Philippians 2:13

~17~
Think About These Things

January 6, 2019

Dear friend,

I wonder if you find, like I do, that there is plenty of room for improvement in your children's behavior. To me, the need for refining feels constant! All day long I am training and correcting and training and correcting, trying to get at the heart of their behavior. I try to stay hopeful in my outlook even while they struggle, fall down, and get back up again. I am watching to see that they will start applying what they have already been taught. I want to be consistent in correcting problem behaviors and wrong ways of thinking. I know I cannot sheepishly wish away the selfish, abrasive ways they can display at times. And so I correct. It takes so much effort and consistency, doesn't it?

On some days, the moments of their challenging behavior feel continual, even if from one child to the next. Once in a while, I can find myself struggling to catch my breath long enough to see something worth encouraging. But I strive to notice the good that I can. I know that I am sharpening my children's Christ-like character by correcting them when it is needed, but I also know that it is equally as important that I encourage their strengths and brighter moments.

As He has in the past, God noticed that I have been feeling this way. Philippians 4:8 had recently caught my attention: "... Whatever is true, whatever is honorable, whatever is just, whatever is pure, whatever is lovely, whatever is commendable, if there is any excellence, if there is anything worthy of praise, think about these things." I knew that my children were doing something helpful, kind, or commendable every day. I didn't want those moments to slip away without being fanned into flame (2 Timothy 1:6). I wanted to find some doable way of paying more attention to my children's genuinely positive traits. God gave me an idea that would help me do that.

The idea God gave me was to create what my family now calls "balloon moments". In the same way that children smile when they see a colorful balloon, God smiles when Van, Liza, Joel, or any of us does something Christ-like: something true, honorable, pure, lovely, or excellent (Philippians 4:8). My family now celebrates those "balloon moments". Many times I simply verbalize their "balloon moment", pointing out what lovely thing they have done and that they have made God smile. On slower days I will trace the outline of a balloon onto a half-sheet of construction paper for each of them and describe with words or pictures what they did that day that made God smile. I let them know that they each had so many "balloon moments" and that I've just chosen one of them.

Liza recently held the front door open for all of us as we headed out of the house in the morning for preschool. She was thinking of others instead of herself, a real accomplishment for a recent 4-year-old, and, praising her, I kissed her and pointed out her "balloon moment". God gave me the clarity in that moment to attribute that moment to her character, calling up that trait to the surface at its first fluttering emergence. "Liza, you are such a helpful girl!", God reminded me to tell her. It felt wonderful to encourage her to see that she was not only doing something helpful but also that she can be someone characterized as helpful.

Van got his coat on without an utterance of frustration and that was a change. "Van, balloon moment! I love how you do not give up!", I told him. Perseverance is a trait we are eager for him to gain. It was so powerful to find and point out a moment when we saw it beginning to bloom.

Joel went to the coat closet and got out his tennis shoes without my asking him to. He grinned ear-to-ear when I noticed his "balloon moment".

In His goodness, God adds to my joy as I encourage my children in living out His ways. His kindness towards me is so deep that as He expands my way of thinking according to His Word, my children are blessed, too.

With love,
Lauren

> "Whatever is true, whatever is honorable, whatever is just, whatever is pure, whatever is lovely, whatever is commendable, if there is any excellence, if there is anything worthy of praise, think about these things."
> Philippians 4:8

†

Lord,

Thank You for delighting in us. We see that You enjoy living closely with us and bringing us all along in Your ways, adults and children alike. Thank You, Lord, that You see the small but important moments and use them to transform us into Your likeness. Thank You that You invite us to celebrate those moments with You!

Quicken our spirits, Lord, to come alive and fill with joy as we step into the character You have designed for each of us so personally. The joy we feel at saying "yes" to Your design for us is incomparable to anything this world can offer. Grow us in Your true, honorable, just, pure, lovely, commendable, excellent, and praiseworthy ways! You are able.

Amen.

Responding:

Day 1

Read Philippians 4:8-9 and write verse 8. In verse 9, we read that we are to "practice" thinking this way. In what way does it encourage you that we get to "practice" thinking this way?

_____

_____

_____

_____

Read Colossians 3:1-2 and write verse 2. What do you think it means to put your mind on "things that are above"? Ask God to help you "set your mind" on your children's strengths today and each day.

_____

_____

_____

_____

Read 1 Corinthians 13:4-7 and write verse 6. Make a habit today of smiling big when you see or overhear your child doing something that makes God smile. That is love rejoicing with the truth alive in your child. What kinds of moments and attributes will you look for and rejoice about? List them here to train yourself to notice them.

Pray: Read over what you have written down in response to today's questions. Close your eyes now and talk honestly with God about what you have written and about what you are thinking and feeling.

Day 2

Read and write Philippians 2:3-4. What are some ways that a child can "count others more significant than themselves"? What would that look like?

Read Psalm 51:7-10 and write verse 10. Do you struggle with any hardheartedness towards one of your children? Bitterness towards someone can keep us from being willing to notice their strengths. List here four positive attributes with which God has blessed the child you have in mind. Ask God to remove any bitterness in your heart.

Watch your children today to notice each of them doing something that makes God smile. Write each of their names below and jot down what you see them do. Then draw a simple balloon shape on a piece of construction paper, cut it out, and write your child's balloon moment on it - whatever he or she did that made God smile. Present it to them at a quiet time of the day when you will have their undivided attention. Tell them it is a moment you noticed today that they did something really special, something that "made God smile". It is not important for the balloon or your handwriting to be beautiful, only that it highlights a behavior or attitude that you want to encourage in your child, and that you get it done!

_____

_____

Pray: Read over what you have written down in response to today's questions. Close your eyes now and talk honestly with God about what you have written and about what you are thinking and feeling.

> *"Love does not rejoice at wrongdoing,*
> *but rejoices with the truth."*
> *1 Corinthians 13:6*

~18~
Dig Deep

February 3, 2019

Dear friend,

When I've given all that I can as a mother, and I feel I am at the end of myself, and then more is asked of me, it matters what I "bring" at that moment. If I want to bring God glory, I have to dig deep, really deep. I must not give my children - or give God in my loving service to Him through mothering - what is on the surface of me: frustration, irritation, fatigue, or anger. I have to choose to dig deep. It doesn't come naturally.

When I am getting to the end of myself and operating out of the fumes that are left, when I'm relying on my reserves, my behavior towards my children tends to worsen. Digging only as deep as my reserves go isn't enough. Instead of bringing my greatest stretching effort, what I need to bring to my aid is God's ability. At the end of myself, I find that God is still there and fully able. He is what is at the deepest part of me; He is my foundation, my God in whom I can completely trust. In my weakest moments, I get to choose to get under the surface of myself, and in the little moments that add up to our days to dig deep and lay the foundation on the rock (Luke 6:48).

I had an unmedicated labor and delivery with our oldest son, Van, and when it came time to push in the last moments, my pushing was not immediately terribly productive. It was very upsetting, to say the least, because it was just so painful and we weren't getting anywhere. After a half hour of unproductive pushing, one of the nurses in my delivery room leaned down to me and, whispering in my ear, advised me quietly and succinctly to "push through to the other side of the pain". I understood her meaning as clearly as a bell. I started pushing through to the other side of the pain, instead of pushing into it and working against it. After a few pushes, out came Van into the world and it was all over.

Now these days, when Van is melting with frustration or tiredness, I know what angle to take: I have to dig deep and *choose* to let God have His way. Again, digging only as deep as my own emotional reserves will not suffice. On my own, I absolutely cannot love as I am called to. But when I dig as deep as my foundation, to God, and I decide to do it His way, I can do what He has said. Jesus Himself said, "Everyone who comes to me and hears my words and *does them* [italics added], I will show you what he is like: he is a man building a house, who dug deep and laid the foundation on the rock. And when a flood arose, the stream broke against that house and could not shake it, because it had been well built" (Matthew 6:47-48).

Digging deep to lay my foundation on the rock, I will not give in to my angry words. I will not grab hold of my son. I will not try to engage with him while he is upset or while I am, either. Those things would only push us further *into* the pain of the moment. Those ways are unproductive.

Instead, I fix my eyes on Jesus in order to push beyond the challenge of the moment. I choose to be silent and to gather my wits, my resolve, and the love with which God fills me. I wait and cool down. I wait for Van to be able to listen again. Waiting on God's leading, I can direct Van resolutely and even patiently. This is Jesus' strength alive in me at my emptiest and at our neediest. "My flesh and my heart may fail, but God is the strength of my heart and my portion forever" (Psalm 73:26). Jesus Himself beared through His own pain, and on the other side of it, was seated at the right hand of God, having secured our relationship with the Father (Hebrews 12:2). He is experienced with the victory gained by pushing through to the other side of the pain.

God refines me in those moments when I decide not to take the problem I am facing with my children into my own hands. Unequipped on my own, and turning to do it Jesus' way, I find that His way truly does work! I can be loving and clear with my children! I do not need to rely on my own feeble strength! My children respond favorably, knowing that despite having misbehaved, they have been met with both necessary truth and grace (John 1:14). God meets the needs of multiple generations at once! Truly Jesus is the way, the truth, and the life in our everyday moments (John 14:6).

My flesh is continually failing, yes, but God is my everlasting rock and I can utterly depend on Him (Isaiah 26:3-4). My part is to build my life on Him by digging deep: by coming to Him, truly hearing His words, and deciding to do them (Luke 6:47). Jesus is my unmovable, unshakable, fully trustworthy Rock.

With love,
Lauren

> "Everyone who comes to me and hears my words and does them, he is like a man building a house, who dug deep and laid the foundation on the Rock."
> Luke 6:47-48

†

Lord,

I know that my human nature offers me no help. But I receive Christ's righteousness from You and find that You make His ways available to me (Romans 4:3). You do exactly what You say You can and will do, putting Your matchless truth and grace on display. You actually push me through the moment and beyond. You use even our most painful moments for Your glory and our good.

I want to say "yes" to You in every little moment and to welcome Your Spirit who brings life. I believe You, my rock, and that You will always supply me with Yourself when I come to You (John 7:38).

Amen.

Responding:

Day 1

Read Luke 6:46-49 and write verse 48. What does it mean to you to "dig deep and lay your foundation on the rock"?

_____
_____
_____
_____

Read and write Psalm 127:1a. What is it that keeps you, in your own most difficult moments, from "letting the Lord build your house"?

_____
_____
_____
_____

Read and write Hebrews 12:1-2. What will you do the next time a frustrating situation arises with your children, in order to "let the Lord build your house"?

_____
_____
_____
_____

Pray: Read over what you have written down in response to today's questions. Close your eyes now and talk honestly with God about what you have written and about what you are thinking and feeling.

Day 2
Read Psalm 18:25-30 and write verse 30. What does this verse teach you about God? How does that encourage you to trust Him?

_____
_____
_____
_____

Read Psalm 18:1-3 and 16-19, imagining our "enemies" as the frustration, anger, and irritation that distract us from keeping our eyes fixed on Jesus. Write verse 19. What would it feel like to let God rescue you the next time you want to do something hard His way?

_____
_____
_____
_____

Read Isaiah 26:3-4. What does it mean to you personally that God is your rock?

_____
_____
_____
_____

Pray: Read over what you have written down in response to today's questions. Close your eyes now and talk honestly with God about what you have written and about what you are thinking and feeling.

"Blessed is the man who remains steadfast under trial."
James 1:12a

~19~
The Lord Disciplines

February 17, 2019

Dear friend,

When I stop to consider it, I find that a lot of my big emotional reactions to my kids' behaviors and to the more harrowing moments of motherhood reflect my fears. In those moments, my thoughts sound like this: "Why is my child not learning this?! Will she ever?! Haven't I actually been teaching this lesson for years?!?!" And then alternately, I'll second guess what the problem manifesting itself is, and I'll wonder, "What if that is what I should be cracking down on, not the other things I've been focusing on with her?!"

In those moments of sudden fear or worry, I try to implement a whole new action plan all of a sudden. I'll abruptly expect my kids to be able to get their shoes and coats on to go out somewhere, without a peep of conversation, for example. When they "fail" to do what I've suddenly decided they must be able to do, I'll come down hard on them for not having met my brand-new, unexplained expectation. Or, for example, thinking that my kids should be able to wait perfectly peacefully for me to be ready to go, without having taught them what that looks like, I'll become exasperated that they "can't" do it. It is often in these moments that my worry about what they can and can't do actually reflects how I am doing as a mother. When I become worried or fearful, I get unnecessarily upset with my children. I speak harshly and unforgivingly. I overpower their confusion with my fear.

At other times, I fear I'll look back one day and wish I would have paid attention to what I should have recognized as red flags. I fear I'll want to ask my older self one day why I didn't do more about "those things". Fears about today impacting tomorrow disrupt my thoughts and lead me to behave equally as immaturely and unwisely.

When I allow any fear to gain my attention, I allow it to eclipse my God-given wisdom. I quickly lose track of how God has told me to go about parenting my children. I stop trusting in all of God's guidance to me and how far it has led us and start instead to lean on my own broken understanding (Proverbs 3:5). I try to take the reins back from God! It's no wonder that I start to scramble and I lose my peace. Separating myself from God even momentarily, I sense how dark it is to live apart from Him. I see what I have done and I am disappointed that I've chosen my own way again. I think to myself, "I knew better!"

The world might say that that feeling of disappointment is only the struggle of a guilty conscience or even a drive for perfection. But I don't agree. I believe that I feel the weight of that disappointment in my behavior at times because it is God's way of disciplining me. I feel the darkness of having turned away from how God has told me to handle something. It feels heavy. My sense of that weight is the consequence I face for having turned away from God's loving instruction for me. I feel the weight of God's dislike for my pride, my thinking I knew better than He does. I know I've done wrong. It stands out in stark contrast to the blessing of life lived His way. This is God's holy discipline of me. God's discipline is gentle and controlled, but it is present.

In our American culture, the word "discipline" is unpopular. It sounds harsh. But God's discipline of us is for our good and it is done in love. He loves me and my children so much that He will not let me go on behaving the way I have. He has a better plan for me than that! His Word says: "God is treating you as sons. For what son is there whom his father does not discipline?... Besides this, we have had earthly fathers who disciplined us and we respected them. Shall we not much more be subject to the Father of spirits and live? For they disciplined us for a short time as it seemed best to them, but he disciplines us for our good, that we may share in his holiness." (Hebrews 12:7, 9-10).

As a loving and faithful father, God does not point out my wrongdoing and then leave me to feel ashamed. The purpose of God's discipline, rather, is to point out to me the darkness of life lived apart from Him and to invite me back into closeness with Him. My experience of Him lines up perfectly with what He has said He will do. He says that He will declare our sins to us: "And if they are bound in chains and caught in the cords of affliction, then He declares to them their work and their transgressions, that they are behaving arrogantly" (Job 36:8-9).

How we respond to His discipline is our choice: "He opens their ears to instruction and commands that they return from iniquity. If they listen and serve him, they complete their days in prosperity, and their years in pleasantness. But if they do not listen, they perish by the sword and die without knowledge" (verses 10-12). Even in my wrongdoing, He keeps on showing me the singularly better way. He is still available to me even when I have turned aside from His instruction. As many as my sins may be, as His repentant child, His mercy towards me is more (Papa 2019).

God's discipline allows me to clearly see the fears that distracted me from His cause and His way. Brought back under His good and wise authority, I see that I must not satisfy my fears. I must not give in to them and their noisy voices. I must instead, right then and there at the moment of their climbing to the surface, choose to continue cooperating with God in His slow, holy way of shepherding my children.

As I follow Him in all my ways, He straightens my path (Proverbs 3:6). I am learning that His way is truly more loving, effective, and transformative than any snap-reaction, emotion-driven response of mine could ever be.

With love,
Lauren

> "But put on the Lord Jesus Christ, and make no provision for the flesh, to gratify its desires."
> Romans 13:14

✝

Lord,

Thank You that You stand ready and available to us always. Even when we have turned aside from You and act out of our own natural way instead of Your holy way, You stay with us and You keep on teaching us. Thank You that even when we are unfaithful to You, You remain faithful to us, Your children, whom You love.

I thank You, Lord, that You correct us. You allow us to feel the weight of sin and darkness when we are not walking closely with You. Your discipline is evidence of Your love for us, because gently but clearly You show us that that is not the way. And then you lead us further on with You.

Lord, You know my fears, You see my grumpy attitude at times, and You are well aware when I am ashamed of having spoken or behaved wrongly towards my children. Would you please purify my heart so that I am completely devoted to You?

And when I experience Your discipline, would You cause me not to grow weary but instead to gladly return to Your ways? Please give me the strength to rise up over the disappointment in how I've behaved and to love my children well, trusting You to take us onward. Your enduring love is my source of hope.

Amen.

Responding:

Day 1

What fears threaten to derail your steady perseverance in God's ways as you mother? List them here. Then read Isaiah 54:17. When you "hear" God declaring this verse to you, how does it make you feel?

_____

_____

_____

_____

Read Job 36:8-12. Is God declaring to you any behaviors or tendencies that He wants you to change? Make some honest notes and thank God for teaching you.

_____

_____

_____

_____

Read and write Romans 13:14. What does it mean to you, as a mother, to "put on the Lord Jesus Christ and make no provision for the flesh"?

_____

_____

_____

_____

Pray: Read over what you have written down in response to today's questions. Close your eyes now and talk honestly with God about what you have written and about what you are thinking and feeling.

Day 2

Read Lamentations 3:19-22 and write verse 22. What do you learn about God from this verse?

_____
_____
_____
_____

Read Hebrews 12:5-6 and write verse 6. Be encouraged that God instructs and corrects His children out of His great love for us. What connection do you see between correction and love?

_____
_____
_____
_____

Read 2 Thessalonians 3:3-5 and write verse 5. From verse 5, what two things will sustain us to continue walking closely with God?

_____
_____
_____
_____

Pray: Read over what you have written down in response to today's questions. Close your eyes now and talk honestly with God about what you have written and about what you are thinking and feeling.

"The steadfast love of the Lord never ceases;
his mercies never come to an end."
Lamentations 3:22

~20~
Pain

March 8, 2019

Dear friend,

When my husband and I were taking a childbirth class leading up to the last trimester of my first pregnancy, we learned an acronym for PAIN. During labor, PAIN is: productive, anticipated, intermittent, and normal. Once labor began, I kept saying the words that form that acronym over and over again to myself, and Jeff would recite them to me, too. Remembering that acronym truly gave me a lot of comfort. I had been afraid that the contractions of labor would feel like something was going wrong, like my body was being terribly damaged. I had been afraid that the contractions would make me feel panicked. But reciting the acronym replaced my inaccurate fears with the truth of what was taking place:

P: Knowing that the contractions and the vivid pain that they brought was actually **productive** in bringing the baby down into my pelvis truly helped me mentally and physically cope with the pain. I had to allow each contraction to do its work in bringing this baby closer to birth. I understood that what I was experiencing was actually moving us closer to the intended goal.

A: The pain I felt was **anticipated**. I had anticipated those contractions for nine months and I knew they would start and then continue until the work was done. I knew that this is what it takes to bring a baby into the world.

I: The pain was **intermittent**, coming and going like waves do.

N: The difficulty of what I was experiencing was **normal**. The pain of it was what every woman who has had an unmedicated childbirth has experienced. This, I knew, was what natural childbirth involves. I knew I needn't be scared; I only had to decide to persevere, mind over matter.

Years later now, as parents of three, my husband and I enjoy retelling our children's birth stories on the night of their birthdays. We have told our children that it takes hard work to birth a baby. Having heard her birth story annually now for four years, our daughter Liza recently told me that as I labored to deliver her, she "said" to me: "Mommy, can you help me out of here?" She envisions labor and delivery as a collaborative effort between mother and daughter. It probably is so, more than I realize.

Now as Jeff and I raise Liza and her brothers, I am still daily "helping them out" through the moments of life they find difficult. In the everyday ups and downs of doing my part to mold my children's character, the PAIN acronym strengthens me to persevere and fix my eyes on the prize of their learning to live closely with Jesus. Now in the midst not of childbirth but of childrearing, the PAIN acronym still applies:

P: The hard moments, the "contractions", that I face with my children now - their spats over who gets which toy, their frustrations with each other's antics, their emotional outbursts over their preferences, their moments of disobedience - they can be **productive**. When I help them respond productively, my children learn from the tough moments they face and apply those lessons to the next challenging moments that arise.

The hardest part for me is that our tougher moments can only be **productive** if I am willing to face them and deal with them in a biblical way. It would be so much easier to brush over the tough moments we face together by either giving my kids what they want or by distracting them with something else. But by doing that, I am just brushing the "pain" of those moments under the rug without really dealing with them. When I do that, my children and I are all missing the valuable lessons that could be learned.

It gets uncomfortable having to handle the hard moments! I feel uncomfortable, for example, when I send Liza to her room because she pushed her baby brother and it won't be allowed. I feel uncomfortable because then she cries and it becomes a whole big emotional moment to walk her through. But when I uphold my expectation that she behave kindly towards her brother, making a point of it with her, isolating that instance so that I get her attention on the matter, that hard moment becomes **productive**. Now what was painful has been useful in teaching her! To my surprise and delight, that tough moment has now brought us closer to the goal of godly character and applying it to real-life, everyday experiences. That pain is productive.

I recently made my youngest, Joel, cry, too, when I corrected him for having spoken angrily at his sister. He is only two years old, and I felt badly for making my little boy upset. That moment felt very uncomfortable to me. But when Joel felt my disapproval, his tears showed me that my reprimand had marked his heart. Because I singled out his misbehavior, he knows what I expect of him and he knows I will uphold that expectation of him. My willingness to point out that difficult moment with him meant that God could use it **productively**.

When my children are uncooperative when Jeff and I are getting them ready for bed, they lose the privilege of a bedtime book. They burst into tears at that rare announcement. That becomes something else my husband and I have to deal with. But the learning that results is worth the discomfort we feel! They learn to cooperate the next night. That pain is productive.

Facing the discomfort that these moments bring is worth the learning my children gain. Not shying away from dealing with the difficult moments, they become memorable and instructive.

A: God **anticipated** that children would need help to learn and grow. The training they require is not a deviation from His plan. He is not surprised when these tough moments arise. We may cringe, but He stands ready. He has **anticipated** these moments and they are a part of His good plan to lead them into godly character. God instructs us as parents to teach our children about living life closely with Him, and on an ongoing basis: "when you sit in your house, and when you walk by the way, and when you lie down, and when you rise" (Deuteronomy 6:7). Yes, God knew that the training we invest in our children would be continual! He knows that "for the moment all discipline seems painful rather than pleasant, but later it yields the peaceful fruit of righteousness to those who have been trained by it" (Hebrews 12:11). God is leading us through these **anticipated** struggles, and we get to trust Him with the results as we follow Him faithfully.

I: As in childbirth, my hardest childrearing moments are **intermittent**, coming and going. The challenges are interspersed regularly with joy, love, laughter, and peace.

N: The fact that my children start and stop and struggle through the development of their character is evidence that they are still children as of yet. They are learning the ropes of life for the first time. It is **normal** for them to struggle as they learn in real time. I need not be concerned as challenges arise; they are a normal part of life and growth. Jesus Himself reminds me that in the world I will have trouble but that nevertheless I must not lose heart, because He has overcome the world (John 16:33).

Like the pain of the contractions involved in my children's births, I believe that the painful moments I face with my children now are definitively producing God's ways in them. Will I submit to God so fully that I actually embrace the painful moments of childrearing?

Can I bear through the pain and let Him use it productively, to produce His life in us?

Can I learn to genuinely appreciate the toughest moments because they have the potential to bring about progress?

If I can learn to embrace those moments, then, surprisingly, I can even be joyful as I walk with God through that hard work He is doing. I yearn to trust Him fully and joyfully (1 Timothy 6:6)!

With love,
Lauren

> "We rejoice in our sufferings, knowing that suffering produces endurance, and endurance produces character, and character produces hope."
> Romans 5:4

✝

Lord,

I thank You that in all of Your plans - childbirth and childrearing included - even pain has purpose. You waste nothing. There is glory for You in everything. There is goodness that arises for our joy and for Your glory even out of tantrums. You call us into the purposefulness of painful moments. Lord, would you please use those tough moments to grow our children's character? That they would not simply muddle through the tough moments, but Lord, actually grow more and more into Your likeness because of them? Would you teach them perseverance when they get frustrated with trying? Lovingkindness and forbearance when they are irritated with their brothers? Contentment when they don't get their way? Would you use those waves of discomfort to "birth" them little by little into the creatures You created them to be?

And, would You please, according to Your design, use the painful moments we mothers experience with our kids to grow our own character? Please use those tough moments to make us more merciful, loving, and wise. We want to display Your character more and more every day. Would you cause us as mothers, Lord, to be able to rejoice in the parenting challenges we face, expecting You to have Your way in our children and in us?

Amen.

Responding:

Day 1

With God, tough moments can be productive. Read Romans 5:3-5 and write verse 3. What are you struggling through with your children that God wants to use productively?

_____

_____

_____

_____

Read and write James 1:12. What valuable outcomes could result from your walking hand in hand with God through the parenting struggle you identified in the previous question? Ask God right now to make you more steadfast in the hard moments.

_____

_____

_____

_____

Read 1 Peter 1:6-7 and write verse 7. How can trusting God through various trials result in glory and honor to Him?

_____

_____

_____

_____

Pray: Read over what you have written down in response to today's questions. Close your eyes now and talk honestly with God about what you have written and about what you are thinking and feeling.

Day 2

Read 2 Corinthians 4:17-18 and write verse 17. What parenting challenges can you start to consider "light momentary afflictions"?

_____

_____

_____

_____

Read Hebrews 12:11 and write it here. Then fill in the below chart to stay motivated to pursue the "fruit" God promises you can expect.

_____

_____

_____

Child's name	Area requiring instruction/correction	The "fruit", or character trait, you can expect God to grow

Read 1 Peter 1:22-23 and write verse 22. Then answer, How would treating your children with "earnest love from a pure heart" allow God to use your children's toughest moments more productively?

_____

_____

_____

Pray: Read over what you have written down in response to today's questions. Close your eyes now and talk honestly with God about what you have written and about what you are thinking and feeling.

> "For the moment all discipline seems painful rather than pleasant, but later it yields the peaceful fruit of righteousness to those who have been trained by it."
> Hebrews 12:11

Reflection

Take time to reflect back on what you and God have been talking through together in entries 11 through 20. Look back through your notes to answer these questions.

❀ What recurring topics and themes do you see showing up?

_____
_____
_____
_____

❀ What stands out to you about those recurring topics?

_____
_____
_____
_____

❀ What do you sense God nudging you to know about Him or about your relationship with Him?

_____
_____
_____
_____

❀ How do you think God wants you to apply what He is telling you?

_____
_____
_____
_____

❀ Tell God what questions you have for Him. Make a note of them here so that you remember what you asked Him and can watch for His direction in response.

_____
_____
_____
_____

❀ Thank God for being very present with you and entering into the details of your everyday life with you.

_____
_____
_____
_____

~21~
BOW

April 20, 2019

Dear friend,

There are a lot of days that my kids' noise and busyness fills my mind and it becomes overwhelming. My mind gets cloudy in those moments and I lose track of my tracks, so to speak. I begin, like a runaway train, to veer off the course that God has set out for me and that I've so passionately agreed I'm on board with. On those days I am easily upset and critical, of myself and of my kids. I see how I persist in my poor attitude, and noticing it just adds to the cloudiness. All along I'm asking God to help me to obey, to cause me to obey. I don't want the fact that I'm overwhelmed to result in my losing my temper with my kids as I try to teach them.

I know that my faith in God is a gift from Him (Ephesians 2:8), and I know that improvements in my attitude and perspective are evidence of the work He is doing in my heart (Psalm 119:32). But I also know that God's authority over me does, nevertheless, require my submission and my actual, in-action agreement to do things the way He has told me to. I know that to live out my faith I have to trust that what He says is right and then actually do things His way. But there are days when my bad attitude is hard to shake and I find it hard to obey!

On one of those recent, ruffling days, during my quiet time with God in prayer and with my Bible while the kids napped, I felt so flustered and weak that I went down onto my knees at my usual praying and reading chair. I felt silly and self-conscious doing it. I looked behind me out the back door and then out the window in the front of the room, to see if any neighbors were going to see me doing this. If they did, how would I explain it? "Are you okay?!", they would ask. Well, despite my awkwardness, I decided that God was prompting me to do it, and so I somewhat sheepishly went down onto my knees and I called out to Him. I spoke out loud in a quiet but desperate I-need-you-and-am-so-convinced-of-You voice that I hear myself using often as I talk to God during naptime. I apologized to Him for my lack of abundant love in action toward my children recently. I asked Him to meet me there in a tangible way and to change me so that I could actually give them the deep love I so want to.

I said all I felt I needed to say, but no more; I didn't see any purpose in going on and on so I just stated the facts and my emptiness and my need for Him and I left it at that. I rose from my knees and sat back down. He immediately dropped three distinct words into my mind. I felt so surprised by how quickly He answered my cry to Him, and by how concretely He did it. The words were in my mind as soon as I was seated. I felt that He said to me:

> Believe.
> Obey.
> Watch.

My breath caught as I realized that those words' first letters spell "BOW". I had felt so certain of the need to bow in that moment. I had wanted to demonstrate with my body the state of my heart. Only God could do all of that, giving me His thoughts and offering me His compassion in a way that so specifically addressed my desperation in that very moment.

I had done this seemingly weird thing, I thought, bowing myself before Him, getting uncomfortable to seek Him. He saw what I did and He read my heart, and He cared that I had done it. He had had tremendous purpose in having prompted me to bow down before Him. Then He called me specifically and personally to believe Him, to obey Him, and to watch for Him to work. It was a moment of communing together and communicating with one another. It was profound and He stunned me.

I learned in that moment, more piercingly than I had known it before, that God is truly with me. I am not alone in the hardest parts of parenting.

I also learned anew that while God does sometimes give me particular steps to take, His overarching answer to my needs is that I walk closely with Him. He asks me to be faithful and expectant. On this occasion, God did not specify a particular action for me to take, a certain message to teach my kids, a certain activity to arrange, or a plan to put into place. Rather, what He did was motivate me to seek Him more and to trust Him more. He responded to my prayer that He cause me to obey, by growing my awe at His nearness to me! More aware of the very reality of His presence with me in my life, I submitted further to Him. In my need, God fixed my eyes more firmly on Him.

God's enduring design and desire is that we believe Him, obey Him, and watch for Him marvelously at work. Jesus taught that the work of God is "that you believe in him whom he has sent", in Jesus Himself, the Son of God (John 6:29). Two thousand years later, today His plan for us is still to believe His resurrected Son and to follow Him closely (Matthew 28:20). We are still to believe, to obey, and to watch. He has never left our side (Matthew 28:20)!

With love,
Lauren

> *"And I will give you a new heart,*
> *and a new spirit I will put within you.*
> *And I will remove the heart of stone from your flesh*
> *and give you a heart of flesh.*
> *And I will put my Spirit in you,*
> *and cause you to walk in my statutes*
> *and be careful to obey my rules."*
> *Ezekiel 36:26*

✝

Lord,

Here I am to respond to You and Your instruction that I "BOW":

Believe, *You said. I do completely believe and see that You are "the way, the truth, and the life" (John 14:6). Repeatedly, I see You present and active in my days. Even in the middle of challenge and darkness, I see You show Yourself starkly bright and good in contrast. Again and again You gently and undeniably say "I Am".*

Obey *what I have taught you, You said. In Galatians 5:6 You teach us that "All that matters is faith working through love." When I live not by my own ability or strength but instead by Your power, I live by Your Spirit. I understand that. Now do it, You said! You remind me to act by Your Spirit, by being hidden in You. You walk very closely with me, making this possible. I want so much to do just what you have told me to do. Even when I falter in action, my heart's desire to follow You closely remains unchanged (Psalm 73:26).*

And now **Watch**, *You said. I sense You urging me to do what You have said to do, so that I can see You at work through me and around me, showing Yourself to be exactly who You say that You are. Your ways are victorious. You teach me to believe, to obey, and to watch to see so. You are who You say You are.*

Lord, as I follow You, You will accomplish Your glory on display. You are always true to Your Word.

Amen!

Responding:

Day 1

Read Matthew 16:15-17 and write Peter's words. If you struggle with any area of unbelief relating to who God is or how He can work in your life, talk with Him openly about that now. You can pray like a parent in the Bible did, with total honesty and heartfelt request: "Lord, I believe; help my unbelief!" (Mark 9:24).

_____
_____
_____
_____

Have you ever felt God trying to slow you down to take a moment to talk with Him? If you have found yourself in great need today, would you consider getting down on your knees to talk with God right now?

_____
_____
_____
_____

Read and write Psalm 34:17-18. By faith, we are "the righteous" the psalmist refers to. Make a list of some of the many means God could use to "deliver you" out of a current challenge in parenting. Watch to see what He will do to address your need.

_____
_____
_____
_____

Pray: Read over what you have written down in response to today's questions. Close your eyes now and talk honestly with God about what you have written and about what you are thinking and feeling.

Day 2

Read Exodus 3:13-14 and write down the name God uses for Himself in verse 14. What does this name mean to you?

_____
_____
_____
_____

Read and write Hebrews 4:12-13. How have you experienced God's Word piercing your heart?

_____
_____
_____
_____

Read and write John 14:23-26 and write verse 23. How would you describe what it means for God to make His home with you?

_____
_____
_____
_____

Pray: Read over what you have written down in response to today's questions. Close your eyes now and talk honestly with God about what you have written and about what you are thinking and feeling.

> "Exalt the Lord our God;
> worship at his footstool!
> Holy is he!"
> Psalm 99:5

~22~
Commit Your Way

May 1, 2019

Dear friend,

God is so kind to teach me and to do it in a way that I perceive and understand! I am certain that He is guiding me. But I am so used to my old ways of doing things that, not meaning to, I sometimes delay in applying His lessons to my life. I thank God that He does not turn away from me when I need to learn a lesson again or hear it from a new angle. He is willing to address all of the facets of the lesson that I require.

Earlier this season, for example, God spoke to me about believing Him, obeying Him, and then watching for His results. When earlier this month I found myself at a place of uncertainty about how to correct and discipline my kids, though, I did not think to apply that lesson - to believe Him, obey Him, and watch for His results in that area. I was unsure how to go forward and I asked God about it specifically instead.

Let me give you some background. Five years ago, when my oldest child was two years old, a mentor of mine shared with me how she had trained and disciplined her children when they were young. Using the metaphor of an umbrella, my mentor taught me to train my children to live "under the umbrella" of God's protection and authority: they are to live His way and so enjoy the closeness of life with Him (D. Sjogren 2018). Since I live under God's umbrella, my children are to live obediently under my "umbrella", too, since God has given me to them to guide them in His ways. I learned to set up clear expectations of obedience for them and clear consequences for when they did not meet them. Most importantly, I learned to try to maintain my composure and my right heart before God so that I correct and teach my children in love and never in anger. A second resource a year later underscored the biblical purpose for disciplining our children: we are to help our children understand how they have moved outside of God's plan when they disobey and restore them back to their good and right place under His loving authority (Tripp 1995).

Thanks to the good guidance I've received, I have had a clear purpose and plan for how to discipline my kids, but nevertheless, the daily challenges have sometimes clouded my vision. That was the case earlier this month when I asked God for guidance about disciplining my kids. I felt discouraged that they kept on showing the same behaviors despite my effort at training them. I felt like I was missing something, but what? I asked God.

God met me on this point when I needed Him to. As I prayed and thought about it that week, I sensed God quieting my search for new answers and giving me peace that I had not missed something essential. He dispelled my doubts and fears and I felt newly clear-minded about going forward. I felt God was telling me to *commit* my way to Him. He wanted me to do what I had already been taught, and to trust Him with the results of that in His timing. In retrospect, I see that it was a clear application of His earlier instruction that I "BOW" (believe, obey, and watch).

God used His Word that week to make sure I felt confident that that was His message for me. I had been reading through the book of Psalms, reading one Psalm each day as my morning devotion reading. As I read that day's Psalm, I shook my head in amazement that He would so directly communicate with me and confirm His message that I "commit" my way to Him. I read:

"Commit your way to the Lord;
Trust in him and he will act.
He will bring forth your righteousness as the light,
And your justice as the noonday.

Be still before the Lord and wait patiently for him;
Fret not yourself over the one who prospers in his way,
over the man who carries out evil devices!

Refrain from anger, and forsake wrath!
Fret not yourself; it tends only to evil.
For the evildoers shall be cut off,
But those who wait for the Lord shall inherit the land."

Psalm 37:5-9

The verbs in those verses of Psalm 37 were for my eyes and ears that day. Taken from those verses, His instructions were for me to: commit, trust, be still, wait patiently, fret not, refrain, and forsake. In my own words, I saw that my role is to commit, to persevere, and to trust. So much trust! I am to be obedient to His instructions to me, and to trust Him with the results. Throughout these verses, I saw the promise of God in action in our lives on our behalf: He will be the one to accomplish His purpose, as I commit to following Him!

As I have applied God's instruction to my thinking about how to discipline my kids, I feel at peace about how to go forward. When, for example, Liza is refusing to stay in her room for naptime, I know to hold the line, with resolve and love. There is no new tactic I must try; I am to apply what I have learned and watch God use that in His timing. When in the past I have wondered how to respond to Van's request to add the "last pieces" of Legos to his creation before coming to breakfast, I now know to hold to my word and expect him to put them down then and come straight away. I realized that there was nothing new to consider in those scenarios and that there was no change required in my thinking about how to handle them. God had already told me how to handle those situations. I was to do exactly that and then expectantly watch for His results. So now I know which way to go when I get to those little, but significant, forks in the daily road. I am to commit my way to Him and the instruction He's given me and watch for Him to handle things from there.

Gentle and kind, God also nudged me to see that motherhood is a *sacred* assignment. He is the one who made me a mother, who formed the children who grew in my womb. My task is inherently of a holy nature, then: it is from Him and for Him. One afternoon during the kids' naptime, I wrote down the word "sacred" in my journal to see where God would lead my thinking. I jotted down what popped to mind:

S - smile
A - affection
C - clear expectations and consistent consequences
RED - the color of extravagant love

I had asked the Lord what element of training I had missed. His response was to motivate and deepen my commitment to Him and His sacred assignment, in full trust that He will do with it what He planned from the beginning. Do you see? We are privileged to live as mothers in His service and under His instruction!

With love,
Lauren

> "Commit your way to the Lord;
> trust in Him and He will act."
> Psalm 37:5

✝

Lord,

As I work to follow You in every area of my parenting, would you please quiet my mind so that I remain committed to Your service? Please remind me of what You have already taught me, and please convict me of my responsibility to live out those plans in submission to You. I trust You to accomplish what You want to. I want to allow You to work through me. Help me please, according to Your Word, to be still, to wait patiently for You, and not to fret! I want to refrain from acting outside of Your plan for me. I want to walk humbly with You as You work in my life and in my children's lives.

I am thankful that You have trusted me to cooperate with You in the sacred task of raising up the next generation of Your disciples. You are my Lord!

Amen.

Responding:

Day 1

Read Psalm 37:5-9 and write verse 5. Then complete the chart below to answer the following questions: What verbs in verse 5 are instructions for you to follow? Add them to the column below marked "What I am to do". By contrast, what do you read that God will do? Add those notes to the chart's righthand column. (Note: To be sure, while our children do sin, let us not consider them the "evildoers" in these verses. The "evildoers" are people who turn away from God.)

_____

_____

_____

_____

What I am to do:	What God will do:

When Pharoah and the Egyptian army had cornered God's people in front of the Red Sea, God's people were facing what seemed impossible. Through Moses, God told His people to trust Him and do what He said. Read Exodus 14:10-20 and write Moses' words from verse 13. What similarities do you see between God's instruction in that Exodus passage and God's instruction in Psalm 37?

_____

_____

_____

Read and write Galatians 2:20. What does it mean to you to let Christ live in you?

_____
_____
_____
_____

Pray: Read over what you have written down in response to today's questions. Close your eyes now and talk honestly with God about what you have written and about what you are thinking and feeling.

Day 2

Reread Psalm 37:5-9. Revisit your answer to the first question from yesterday's response questions. Of the things that we are to do, which one is the hardest for you to obey? Why?

_____
_____
_____
_____

Read Psalm 33:13-22 and write verse 20. Who is the answer to all of our challenges and needs?

_____
_____
_____
_____

Read Psalm 139:23-24. Write verses 23 and 24. In what way do you desire to be more fully committed to following Jesus in your motherhood?

_____
_____
_____
_____

Pray: Read over what you have written down in response to today's questions. Close your eyes now and talk honestly with God about what you have written and about what you are thinking and feeling.

> "I have been crucified with Christ.
> It is no longer I who live,
> but Christ who lives in me.
> And the life I now live in the flesh
> I live by faith in the Son of God,
> who loved me and gave himself for me."
> Galatians 2:20

~23~
Simplicity and Godly Sincerity

May 16, 2019

Dear friend,

God has continued to be patient and gentle with me after teaching me earlier this season to "BOW": to believe, to obey, and to watch for Him at work. He keeps showing me how to apply my faith in His sovereignty to so many nuanced areas of my life. One particular area into which God has continued to shine His light is my thought life.

As committed as I am to following God, I find my naturally busy mind working as if it intends to take over, as if it knows more or better than God. My mind's tendency is to overthink things and to imagine that I need to be able to anticipate the countless variables affecting our daily decisions. Regrettably, it is my natural tendency to try to control our circumstances. I fear I must meet all of the day's demands with excellence. This tendency causes me to get stuck in my own head, and I become distracted from the beautiful simplicity of happily carrying out what God has told me to do. Many times, before I realize it, I have been more present with my self-doubts and with evaluations of my performance than I have with the circumstances and people right in front of me. Even recognizing this about myself, I have a hard time turning it off.

God heard my busy mind getting carried away and pointed out a remedy as only He can. As you know, He had recently gotten my attention with Psalm 37. Reading those verses again this week hit me in a new way. In Psalm 37, through His servant David, God provides an important command about living a life of trust in Him. We are to "trust in the Lord and do good; [to] dwell in the land and befriend faithfulness" (3). As I read that, I heard, in a profound way, that God wants for us to follow Him wholeheartedly, and to faithfully and peacefully live out that trust in Him. He wants that so much for us that in Psalm 37:3 He allowed David to give it to us as a command!

God's command to us is simple and straightforward. What a breath of fresh air for me and my striving mind! Like a knowing, loving Father who puts His strong but gentle hand on my shoulder to get my attention, God gave me a nudge as I read David's words. He used those words to tell me to settle down, to rest my mind, to quit my striving. Go faithfully about the work I have given you to do, He said. I had the sense that He was effectively, and yet tenderly, whispering "Shhhhhh" to my mind. God used Psalm 37:3 to give me His profound authorization to go about my work peacefully and contentedly under His command. I need not be in control but rather to trust Him.

Generously, God also directed my attention through my daily Bible reading to 2 Corinthians 1:12, where the apostle Paul declared, "For our boast is this, the testimony of our conscience, that we behaved in the world with simplicity and godly sincerity, not by earthly wisdom but by the grace of God, and supremely so toward you". As I read that verse, it nearly leapt off of the page and onto my lap. I saw that in Jesus I am released to behave with simplicity and godly sincerity; I can have full, undivided mental presence in my responsibilities! I can be faithful and sincere in my mothering, and that is enough for Him! I need not evaluate my "doing" according to any fears that creep up or any worldly wisdom. I get to do this life of faithful mothering His way, thanks to His undeserved love and peace that flows into and through me (John 7:37-38). What sudden, deep, lasting mental freedom He gave me that day.

Agreeing with Him, I am learning to loosen my reins of control over my family's day. I am no longer regularly striving and exerting unnecessary emotional and mental effort. Instead, I am allowing myself to simply be faithful in the tasks and interactions that comprise my day. Who am I to try to manage what is under God's control and command? I may go about my part with "simplicity and godly sincerity".

God uses our faith-filled, expectant reading of His Word to bring light and life to our everyday life. Thanks to His meeting me in His Word on the particular days that He did, I am free - most days - from over-thinking things. I am free from the need to get everything just right the first time. I am free from feeling the pull to satisfy all of my children's emotional needs. I can rest my mind on the truth that He is in control and in charge and that I get to act accordingly. A relief all over! By His power, I can in fact "trust in the Lord and do good" and be satisfied that that is enough for me and for Him (Psalm 37:3a). I can be well as I "dwell in the land and befriend faithfulness" (Psalm 37:3b). I can "behave in the world with simplicity and godly sincerity" (2 Corinthians 1:12) and supremely so towards my family.

God was kind to show me that not only am I free from trying to control my family's day, but the Lord commands me to step back from that effort. My constant controlling pushes God out. If I am going to follow Him fully, my exhausting, demanding thoughts and concerns must quiet down and cease. He deserves the fullness of my attention and cooperation. I am thankful to be peacefully and simply in His service.

With love,
Lauren

> *"For our boast is this, the testimony of our conscience, that we behaved in the world with simplicity and godly sincerity, not by earthly wisdom but by the grace of God, and supremely so toward you."*
>
> **2 Corinthians 1:12**

†

Lord,

You are continually aware of my thought life. You do not enter into my mind and speak to me with condemnation. No, You treat me gently. When You see my mind going astray, You enter in and You whisper Your way to me. You quiet my mind, and You show me that it is for my good and Your glory that You do it.

Thank You, Lord, that You speak to me through Your holy, living Word. You are effective in getting my heart's full attention. Use Your Word to guide me as a mother in my everyday life with my family. I ask You to cause me to trust You with the day that You have provided. Would you bring my mind into regular submission to You, as I attend sincerely to the people and tasks You've given me? I want to live faithfully and simply in Your service.

Amen.

Responding:

Day 1
Read Psalm 139:1-6 and write verse 5. What thoughts or concerns distract you from mothering? Pray that God will deal with them as you release them to Him.

_____

_____

_____

_____

Read and write Psalm 37:3. What does it mean to you to be a mother who "dwells in the land and befriends faithfulness"? Have you considered before how valuable your faithfulness in mothering is to God?

Read and write 2 Corinthians 1:12. How would behaving with "simplicity and godly sincerity" change how you think today? How would it change how you behave?

Pray: Read over what you have written down in response to today's questions. Close your eyes now and talk honestly with God about what you have written and about what you are thinking and feeling.

Day 2
Read Galatians 5:1 and write it here. From what thought patterns would you like to ask God to free you?

Read Psalm 19:7-11 and write verse 7. In what ways has following God recently been "reviving to your soul"?

Read Psalm 46:10 and copy it here. What is one way that you can begin to train yourself to "be still" and to trust what God is up to?

_____

_____

Pray: Read over what you have written down in response to today's questions. Close your eyes now and talk honestly with God about what you have written and about what you are thinking and feeling.

"The law of the Lord is perfect, reviving the soul."
Psalm 19:7

~24~
In Deed and In Truth

May 25, 2019

Dear friend,

I love to teach my children about God. It is one of my favorite things to do, and our family devotion time over breakfast is often my favorite part of the day. When I was young myself, my mom and dad sought to teach me and my brother to love the Lord our God with all our heart, soul, mind, and strength (Deuteronomy 6:5). Now it is one of the greatest joys of my life to try my best to teach my children how to walk closely with Jesus all throughout their days.

I find that teaching my children to follow Jesus involves both word and action. The "word" part of the equation comes more easily for me: I love reading their children's Bibles with them and memorizing Bible verses to tunes with them. I love praying with them and seeing their prayer life develop. I love discussing with them how Jesus wants us to handle the situations we encounter and to shine His light in the world.

I desire with all my heart to couple the teaching and discussion we have about Jesus, the "word" part of the equation, with equally compelling action: I want my behavior towards my children to show them what God's love is like. I don't want to talk about Jesus with passion but fail to let my relationship with Him make me a reliably loving mother. I want my love for Jesus and my reliance on Him to so overpower my human nature that I can love them in a way that resembles something of how Jesus loves us. I also want them to see the very real impact He has on our ability to love each other in action.

But, while my spirit is willing, my flesh is weak (Matthew 26:41). I find I can resolve in one moment to show my children nothing but love ever again, but then a moment later the bubble breaks and there I am again, all upset and rattled by something one of them has said or done. I know my feelings are natural. But I also know that God does not want me to be controlled by my emotions. He instructs us: "Let every person be quick to hear, slow to speak, slow to anger; for the anger of man does not produce the righteousness of God" (James 1:19-20). We are intended, as followers of Jesus, not to love in word or talk, but in deed and in truth (1 John 3:18).

God has been aware of the tension I've felt between wanting to love well, on one hand, and experiencing my inability to do it consistently, on the other. Recently, He used a Bible study I am in to shed His light into this area.

As I worked on my Bible study homework, I read about Jesus going from town to town and spending time with people who are sick, afflicted, confused, and helpless (Matthew 9). His response to them and their many physical, emotional, and spiritual needs was pure, wholehearted compassion. His response to people's neediness was not anger or frustration. He knew that every bit of their neediness reflected their need for their heavenly Father (Matthew 9:35-38; Psalm 23:1). Jesus used the opportunities presented by the people's needs to meet their physical needs and also to teach them many things of eternal value (Mark 6:34). He saw the people "like sheep without a shepherd" (Mark 6:34b), in deep need of our heavenly Father in every aspect of life. Jesus' love for God the Father directly impacted how He related to the people in His life. Jesus loved the Father enough to do what He said to do, and so the Father's generous and merciful love for the people flowed through Jesus (John 14:31).

God used Jesus' example in those passages from the gospel accounts to soften my heart towards my children and their neediness. He taught me that my own children approaching me with their needs are much like the people who approached Jesus with theirs. Like the people Jesus met, my children are like sheep in need of their Shepherd. They require His attention and compassion in every facet of their lives. They will be satisfied only by His love and care. Because I seek to follow Him as I mother, every bit of their neediness is an opportunity for me to address their physical needs and to point them to their heavenly Father. I can grow in my ability to love my children well by watching and studying Jesus' example.

God showed me through those accounts that He wants my heart as their mother to be like Jesus' heart in those moments: gentle and compassionate towards them. I can grow in my ability to love my children well by asking God to give me His heart for my children. As a result, now I am asking God to cause me to see them through His eyes, the way Jesus saw the people He met face to face. I want to feel His compassion towards them and to understand their perspective on the things that upset them. I ask God to cause me to feel genuinely more patient, gentle, and willing to instruct them, and then to cause me to follow through accordingly.

God wants my love for Him to overflow into love in action, just as Jesus' did and continues to do today. In the last chapter of the book of John, the risen Christ repeatedly asks the disciple Peter whether Peter loves Him. Peter insists that he does. Jesus' response is to tell Peter to "tend [His] sheep" (John 21:16) and to "feed [His] sheep" (John 21:17). Jesus intends for our love for Him to produce tender, loving care in action for His people. Jesus instructs us "so that [we] will love one another" with His love (John 15:17). I am newly convicted that one of my great purposes is to love in Jesus' name, and that conviction drives my behavior.

Looking at Jesus, I conclude that:
- He is my example of love in action.
- My children and their neediness require God's love in action.
- God Himself softens my heart towards my children as I ask Him to.
- Jesus' love in action towards me is what fills and satisfies me so that I can overflow with His love towards my family (Psalm 23:5).
- I have been given the assignment of loving in Jesus' name (John 13:34-35).

In summary, my ability to love my children well - in action - is entirely dependent on Jesus from every angle! My ever-growing faith in Jesus is the only source of my ever-growing ability to love. I know that even as much as Jesus leads me, I will still love my children imperfectly. And yet I fully anticipate that my children will grow to see that it is Jesus who has been the source of all of my love all along. I remain steadfast and immovable because my work done in the Lord is never in vain (1 Corinthians 15:58). Even as I stumble in living out His love in action, I am committed to rising again with my eyes fixed on Him (Proverbs 24:16).

With love,
Lauren

> "Little children, let us not love in word or talk but in deed and in truth."
> 1 John 3:18

✝

Lord,

You know that I love You and that I take great joy in introducing You to my children day after day. As I teach them from Your Word, I do it with passion!

I also desire to show them Your consistently compassionate and tender love in action, by my example. But my flesh fails me! Nevertheless, You remain the strength of my heart and my portion forever (Psalm 73:26). I trust You to see my faith in You and to provide in this area of need of mine. In Your abundant grace towards me, You share Your ways with me. Please fill my heart with Your abundant love for each of my children and equip me to love them well in action - in deed and in truth. Glorify Your name to them through me! With love for You, I ask these things.

Amen.

Responding:

Day 1

Read Matthew 9:35-36 and Mark 6:30-34 and notice Jesus' attitude towards the people around Him. What can you learn from Jesus' example in these passages and apply to your motherhood?

_____
_____
_____
_____

Read 1 Thessalonians 2:7-8. Paul's words show us that God wants us to teach our children the gospel and also to give them compassionate, tender care. Which do you find harder: teaching your children about Jesus or showing them tender, loving care? Why do you think that is?

_____
_____
_____
_____

It is God who grows our capacity to love the people around us. Read 1 Thessalonians 3:12. Write that verse here, but replace the word "you" with your own name and replace the words "one another" with your children's names.

_____
_____
_____
_____

Pray: Read over what you have written down in response to today's questions. Close your eyes now and talk honestly with God about what you have written and about what you are thinking and feeling.

Day 2

Read and write 2 Timothy 4:2. From these verses, what two attitudes should characterize our parenting even during the times we must correct our children?

_____
_____
_____
_____

Jesus instructed His disciples to care for His "sheep" out of love for Him. Read John 21:15-17. What kind of love and spiritual food do you "feed" your children? Do you sense Jesus leading you to "feed" your children in some new way?

_____
_____
_____
_____

Read 1 Peter 5:2-4 and write verse 3. In what area of your character would you like to become more of an example to your flock?

_____
_____
_____

Pray: Read over what you have written down in response to today's questions. Close your eyes now and talk honestly with God about what you have written and about what you are thinking and feeling.

"Jesus said to him, 'Feed my sheep.'"
John 21:17

~25~
Completion

July 25, 2019

Dear friend,

One day earlier this week, I started out the day feeling weary, before I even got out of bed. Feeling the weight of the parenting challenges I knew the day would hold, I was disheartened at the get-go. I knew already that I would have a hard time living out my best intentions in the face of the situational challenges I would surely face. The day felt like it would require more emotional fortitude than I expected to be able to bring to it.

I don't mean to paint a dramatic picture of myself. I am generally capable and I always do my best to rise to the challenge as I lean on Jesus. I don't mean to paint a dramatic picture of my children, either. They are enormously special, loving, thoughtful, helpful, creative, joyful, and full of faith. But like all kids, they also get loud, they get upset, they express their preferences, and they argue. They're wonderful kids with the usual emotions, needs, and frustrations, but it can feel like a lot to manage with grace.

I lay in bed that morning before opening my eyes and asked God to incline my heart to Him (Psalm 119:36). To please cause Himself to be so much the focus of my mind that those situational challenges pale in comparison to my clarity and strength in being His servant. I asked Him to restore my ebbing strength and joy.

Just prior to that day, my family and I had returned from two weeks away visiting family out of town. It had been a challenging week settling back into our usual routine at home. Other additions like Vacation Bible School and big yard projects were stretching us even further.

A few hours into our day, on the morning I woke up feeling overwhelmed, my two older children, Van and Liza, were getting along and playing so nicely together upstairs. They had made an imaginary birthday party with blankets on Liza's bedroom floor, little toys all lined up, and animals dancing at the party. They invited me and Joel upstairs as guests to the party. What a peaceful time! They were doing exactly as I have always hoped for them. They were playing happily together, as true friends. They'd chosen an appropriate activity for that time of the day, nothing too boisterous for right after breakfast. They also were fully content. Well done, Van and Liza! But even so, that special moment wasn't without its challenges. There were still frustrations, little things: Joel still bucking his body against me on my lap, crying as the party ended; Van's voice being louder than desirable; the upset to everyone of having to end the party to accommodate our plans for the day. The room was messy with things scattered all around. In short, I guess, it was imperfect, not neat and right from start to finish.

I felt then, and often feel, the tension between the almost perfect success of those moments and still, the imperfection of them. I sense my "new creation" self enjoying the moment, the me who by God's grace sees Him as the source of those special moments when my children share friendship and make good choices. But I regret that at the same time, my "former", lingering self is still so annoyingly present with frustrations, irritations, and the desire for all of it to line up according to my highest expectations. I want to live perpetually as my new creation self, seeing our moments with only holy eyes and a pure heart. I don't want to feel the pull of my frustrations, but the fact is that they still remain, irritating me and disturbing my vision to live fully and completely for God (Romans 7:22-23). I am reminded that I am a work in progress.

After settling Joel down for his nap and moving the big kids downstairs after the "birthday party", I sat down with God at my kitchen table. I asked Him for His refreshment for me before the rest of the imperfect day was to get underway. As I sat talking with Him, He gently brought to my mind the idea that the tensions that I feel - the imperfections in special moments and my inability to live completely purely - are a part of this life and will remain that way until He has truly made all things perfectly new (Revelation 21:5). He gave me peace in realizing that those imperfections are part and parcel of this fallen world. He reminded me that until He restores heaven and earth, the gaps between our existence now and the full life we will have in Him in eternity are a part of His plan. We cannot possibly do enough ourselves to reach His holiness. The gaps in life exist to show that we require His redemption in full.

So it is okay, He showed me, to feel that tension in myself. It is He who will make all things new. It will not be me or my efforts that make myself new or that make my children new. The renewal He brings is continually and exclusively His doing, from start to finish. One day our renewal will be complete and sufficient and perfect. But that will be later. On a date of His choosing, not mine.

I saw that morning that God does not require perfection of any of us. He does not expect circumstances here to reflect Him perfectly. He knows we are incapable of following and reflecting Him unwaveringly. It is why He sent Jesus (Isaiah 59:16). Does my imperfection invalidate God's plan for His glory? No! "I do not nullify the grace of God, for if righteousness were through the law, then Christ died for no purpose" (Galatians 2:21). The Father sent Jesus to restore unholy me to holy God.

Jesus has already come to be the solution to our failings! I get to accept His offering for what I cannot pay for myself.

Most graciously, God showed me that if I am leaning on Him, He is already at work making me new *now*. As I stand in His presence, He is transforming me little by little, imparting His radiance to me (2 Corinthians 3:18). It is not up to me to perfect myself. It is God who relentlessly bridges the gap between my human weakness and my desire to be fully His. I am confident that "He who began a good work in [me] will bring it to completion at the day of Jesus Christ" (Philippians 1:6).

In the meantime, it is immensely freeing to learn that even my imperfection shows how great He is! Even the tensions between my vision for a holy life and the messiness of everyday mothering point to Jesus.

The author and perfecter of my faith is worthy of my devotion in the midst of the messiness of everyday mothering life. I will continue to say "yes" to Him and His good plan moment by little moment. Even on every messy day "I will bless [Him] and praise [His] name forever and ever. Great is the Lord, and greatly to be praised, and his greatness is unsearchable" (Psalm 145: 2-3).

With love,
Lauren

> *"And I am sure of this, that he who began a good work in you will bring it to completion at the day of Jesus Christ."*
> *Philippians 1:6*

✝

Lord,

You give me eyes to perceive Your glory amidst the imperfections of my days. And then when those imperfections begin to disappoint me, You cause me to see that You are aware of them, too, and that they are a part of Your plan.

Even in the imperfections of life I see that You are better than what this life has to offer and that You have been and will continue to be the solution to this fallen world.

When I perceive Your sovereignty in the upsetting, messy everyday moments, I feel free. You accept my insufficiency and You claim the victory through it. As I walk hand in hand with You, You are winning in all of the little moments that will add up to Your complete, finished work one day.

As You teach me these things, Lord, You make me smile. You restore my sense of awe and joy in You. This week You gave me that renewed joy on the day when I woke up so very weary. I did not expect the new strength that You gave me to come on that same day! Oh, how You provide! You know my thoughts and my needs, and You meet me right there.

Lord, by Your power, may I rest into You continually. Help me to live with eyes of faith and to accept Your grace for me and for my children. Thank you for the freedom I have in You and only You, Almighty Father.

Amen.

Responding:

Day 1

When in your day do you find that you notice the tensions between your vision for your family's life and the imperfect realities of life? What feelings do those moments stir up in you?

_____
_____
_____
_____

God claims us as His own but He does not stop there: He is continually actively working in us and drawing us closer to Himself. Read Hebrews 12:1-2. From verse two, what are two of the functions or roles Jesus plays in our faith journey?

_____
_____
_____
_____

Revisit 2 Corinthians 3:17-18 from earlier in your study, and write verse 18. What does it mean to you to meet with God "with unveiled face"?

_____
_____

Pray: Read over what you have written down in response to today's questions. Close your eyes now and talk honestly with God about what you have written and about what you are thinking and feeling.

Day 2
Read and write 2 Corinthians 5:17. What "new" work is God doing in you lately?

_____
_____
_____
_____

Read and write Philippians 1:6. Does knowing that God will bring you to completion one future day give you a sense of freedom from imperfection? Describe what you feel.

_____
_____
_____
_____

It is helpful to me to distinguish between how I think and act when I am behaving as my "old self" as compared to how I think and act when I am exercising my new identity in Christ. (We receive our new identity when we decide to submit to God's authority over us and believe that He redeemed us through His Son, Jesus.) My old self is self-serving, but my new self finds life in God. Complete the below chart to explore any changes you notice God bringing about in you through Jesus. I have included a few examples:

I used to... (My old self)	As a new creation, I... (My new self in Christ)
...squeeze in too much activity out of fear our day won't be fun enough.	... leave margin in our day.
... try to fix the moment quickly.	... take a calmer teaching approach to bring about more heart-level learning.
... deal with my children in the time of my anger.	... wait to discipline my kids until I can do it in a way that honors God.

Pray: Read over what you have written down in response to today's questions. Close your eyes now and talk honestly with God about what you have written and about what you are thinking and feeling.

> "Behold, I am making all things new...
> these words are trustworthy and true."
> Revelation 21:5

~26~
Your Example

August 12, 2019

Dear friend,

Earlier this summer my husband and I had been wrestling with how to get our kids to do what we have taught them to do in the routine, transitional moments of the day. When we call them in from the backyard for lunch, for example, we want them to come in peacefully, to put their shoes away without a big to-do, and to wash their hands for lunch. We've always taught them to do these things. Now that they have been taught, we want them to do it without our having to walk them through each step of it each time. Instead of following our good plan, the boys had been coming in loud and rowdy and would start wrestling just inside the back door. Often it meant someone would get hurt during that transition time from outside to lunchtime. I didn't perceive what they were doing as egregious, but it was a regular disruption to our peaceful day. They were behaving similarly during our regular bedtime routine and when getting from lunch to afternoon quiet time. They were knowingly ignoring our expectations at all of those transitional moments. It left Jeff and I repeatedly reacting to their behavior, even though we had intentionally trained them otherwise. I didn't want to nag them through those transitions, but I was afraid to come down too hard on them. I felt so frustrated by the frequency of the issue that I didn't think I would handle it lovingly. In retrospect, I wish we had come down harder on them. But the reality is that we didn't. I felt unsure of how to handle this recurring issue. So one day I asked God: "What should I do about this? Please tell me clearly."

That afternoon I opened my Bible to continue my daily Bible study homework. I soon came to the 20th chapter of the book of Ezekiel. It is titled "Israel's Continuing Rebellion". Would you believe that God used those three words to grab my attention? I inhaled suddenly when I read them, sensing that God would use these verses to directly answer what I had been asking Him. In the passage, God spoke through his servant Ezekiel to teach some of the leaders of His people, Israel. God reminded them that He had a perfectly good plan for them and that He was leading them toward its culmination (Ezekiel 20:5). But, despite His love, instruction, and promise, His people had directly rebelled against Him by continuing in their old, idolatrous ways (Ezekiel 20:8a).

God was angry and outraged! They had defied Him to His face (Ezekiel 20:8b). He wanted to let them have it, so to speak. But He didn't do that! Instead, God declared that He would deal with His people "for [His] name's sake, not according to [their] evil ways, nor according to [their] corrupt deeds" (Ezekiel 20:44). Again and again He emphatically declared His mercy towards them "for the sake of [His] name" (Ezekiel 20: 9, 14, 17, 22, 44). Yes, He required their holiness and He would follow through with necessary and significant consequences (Ezekiel 20:37). But, He would not exact the full penalty that their sin deserved. Instead, He would deal with them in a way that upheld the righteousness of His name. He would deal with them with truth and also grace (John 1:14).

God opened the eyes of my heart as I read about that response to His people and He used it to answer my question about how to respond to my own children's continuing rebellion during transition times:

In my own way, I feel indignation towards my children, like God did towards His, when they meet my pure-hearted expectations with defiance. Through that passage in Isaiah, God showed me that my desire for my children's holiness mirrors His desire for our holiness. I am right to feel such discomfort in the face of their sin. I am not wrong to hunger and thirst for their righteousness (Matthew 5:6). I am supposed to want them to live according to God's way. God uses my desire for their holiness to fuel me to train my children into godly ways and out of ungodly ways (Proverbs 6:20). Through this passage, I learned that I am right to correct them in everyday moments of rebellion.

By His example in the book of Ezekiel, God also showed me that I am right to implement consequences in order to effectively train my children. His example showed me that the consequences I implement must serve to uphold the righteousness of God's name; they must not serve to make my children "pay" for their misdeeds. God intends for me to respond to my children's rebellion in a way that marks their hearts and leads them to an attitude of genuine repentance and awareness of the life we have only in living closely with God (Ezekiel 20:40, 43).

Now, when my boys come in from the backyard loud and rowdy, I send them back onto the deck and allow them to come in one at a time when they can do it right. If they are not at the table in time for prayer over lunch, they sit on the hallway steps until I sense their readiness to behave according to our expectations. Occasionally they eat alone if they are not "under my umbrella" behaving as we expect them to. God's example gave me surety in my desire for their good behavior and right attitudes as well as surety in implementing consequences. He allowed me to see that He wants me to be full of both truth (upheld expectations and consequences) and grace (more kindness than they deserve) (John 1:14), and not one to the exclusion of the other.

Jesus' example from the 42nd book of Isaiah also instructs me in my motherhood. In those verses, God the Father is describing His Son, Jesus. He paints us a vivid picture of Jesus responding to sin with tremendous faithfulness, truth, and grace: when Jesus restores heaven and earth one day, He will bring justice to all nations and as He does so "He will not cry aloud or lift up his voice, or make it heard in the street" (v. 2) and "a bruised reed he will not break" (v. 3). In accomplishing His divine purpose, Jesus will be powerful and yet gentle. Jesus will act not out of anger but instead out of purity.

As described in Isaiah 42, Jesus will accomplish His work "faithfully" (v. 3). He will be immovable as He perseveres and brings His work to completion. "He will not grow faint or be discouraged" as He does so (v. 4). In His eternal desire to magnify the Father's glory, Jesus will be undeterred. He will be successful in establishing justice. People at His mercy will even wait for His perfect justice, expecting nothing less from Him (v. 4).

If I am to follow Jesus then, as I deal with sin, I must do as Jesus does and will do. Like Him, I am to be faithful, immovable, purpose-driven, and full of the Father's love as I carry out the work He has given me in training my children. Like Jesus, I must never deal with them in the time of my anger (v. 3). Like Jesus, I must press on in my work and faithfully pursue my children's holiness (v. 4). In time, I can even expect my children to learn to wait for the consequences they know will follow rebellious behavior (v. 4). In time, they will come to appreciate the goodness of peaceful transitions all throughout our day.

God is so instructive towards us! In Isaiah 30:18 we read that He "waits to be gracious to [us] and therefore He exalts himself to show mercy to [us]". God does not jump in and smack our hand when we misbehave. He waits in order to be gracious towards us in His discipline. He restrains His anger and holds back the full fire we deserve. He desires to show mercy towards us and so He does. As His child, I can follow His example in that way, too. I must not act in response to the passions of my mind or my flesh, shouting at my kids or otherwise dealing with them in the time of my anger. My children will be blessed by my waiting to deal with them until I can gently and yet firmly address the issue at hand.

God's Word says that "blessed are all those who wait for him" (Isaiah 30:18) and as always, His Word proves true.

With love,
Lauren

> "Therefore the Lord waits to be gracious to you,
> and therefore he exalts himself to show mercy to you.
> For the Lord is a God of justice;
> blessed are all those who wait for him."
> Isaiah 30:18

✝

Lord,

Thank You that You are always incrementally adding to my understanding of Your ways. You teach me when I am in need. You teach me when I am ready to hear from You. You teach me in ways I can perceive! Even though Your ways are so much higher than mine (Isaiah 55:9), You share Yourself with me. What kindness towards me! Thank You specifically for giving me confidence to respond to my children's rebellion and to impose appropriate consequences.

Lord, You see how I strive to impress Your ways upon my children. I desire their holiness, that they would love Your ways. Would You grant me this desire of my heart? I know they will continue to make mistakes, but would You speak into their hearts an irrevocable devotion to You? Allow them, I ask, to gain the full satisfaction of the life found only in following You.

Lord, I want to follow Your example as I train my children. By the power of Your Spirit alive in me, I want to be full of both grace and truth in the parenting moments that are toughest for me. Please cause me, Lord, to trust You so fully that I walk in Your steps faithfully and expectantly.

Amen!

Responding:

Day 1

Read Ezekiel 20:5-17 and write down as many words as you can find that demonstrate how God restrained His anger. How will you follow God's example from these verses?

_____
_____
_____

Read Isaiah 42:1-4 and write verses 2-3a. What part of Jesus' example in these verses inspires you in your mothering, and why?

_____
_____
_____
_____

In Isaiah 42:1-4, we hear twice that God's servant, Jesus, will bring forth justice (verses 1b and 3b). Write verse 3b. Would you say that you are faithful to deal with problematic behaviors and attitudes from your children when they arise? How does Jesus' example in these verses motivate you to address difficult situations more directly?

_____
_____
_____
_____

Pray: Read over what you have written down in response to today's questions. Close your eyes now and talk honestly with God about what you have written and about what you are thinking and feeling.

Day 2
Read James 1:5-8 and write verse 5. In what particular area are you in need of God's wisdom this week or this season?

___

Read Psalm 6:1-2 and write verse 2 here. In these verses, we can see ourselves as the child who has been rebellious towards her heavenly Father. How does it make you feel to realize that God has shown you mercy and healing, helping you even though you have behaved rebelliously towards Him?

___

Read and write John 1:14. What would it look like for you to parent with both grace and truth?

___

Pray: Read over what you have written down in response to today's questions. Close your eyes now and talk honestly with God about what you have written and about what you are thinking and feeling.

> "For my name's sake I defer my anger,
> for the sake of my praise I restrain it for you."
> Isaiah 48:9

~27~
His Desires

September 28, 2019

Dear friend,

I have a prayer schedule that I usually follow, praying for a different group of people in my life on each day of the week: I pray for close friends on Mondays, my Bible study group members on Tuesdays, my family on Wednesdays, and so on. Each day I also pray for anyone who has specifically asked for prayer that week. Having a day designated for each group keeps me committed to praying for the various people I want to pray for, and it keeps me focused (and not overwhelmed by where to start and stop) when I sit down to pray.

Recently it was my day to pray for my family. Sitting down at my kitchen table during my kids' naptime, I began to pray for my children individually, about the particular areas in which I perceive each needs God's help. I often ask God to equip Van with self-control beyond his years and with perseverance to get through hard tasks. I ask God to help Liza gain control over the strong emotions that try to disturb her peace and contentedness. I ask God to give Joel a spirit of kindness and to quiet his quick temper. After covering their individual needs that day though, I felt a pressing desire to pray for their faith and so I continued praying for them longer than I had intended to.

As I prayed, suddenly I felt such clarity and boldness and deep faith in what I was praying for them! My prayers no longer felt like requests. They felt like promises from God that I was claiming for them! I felt that God reached in and ordered my prayers, fanning them into flame and seconding them with His passion. My prayers felt concrete and distinct and inspired. It felt like God and I were praying together. This was a new experience for me and it grabbed my attention the way a strong, sudden wind does. Do you know the kind of wind that is so sudden, swirling, and powerful that it causes you to stop what you are doing and look up and see the trees moving and swaying from side to side? It is so strong that you feel like you can almost see it. The Holy Spirit was moving in my prayer in the same powerful way (Acts 2:2)!

I learned that day in a new, profound way that God not only participates with us in the practical, everyday matters of mothering, but that He is truly and powerfully acting in our children's lives and hearts *in deep spiritual matters*. He uses prayer to affect the practical, everyday matters of life. He saw my love for my children and my trust in Him, and He filled my love and faith with more of His Holy Spirit.

Psalm 37:4 says that when we delight ourselves in the Lord, He will give us the desires of our hearts. He saw my delight and my trust in Him, and He joined in with my prayer in a way that made His desires for my children to be my desires for my children. Full of His Holy Spirit, I got to pray for my children what God wants for my children! He was not saying yes to whatever I asked, but rather making what He wants for my children into what I want for my children! He is working to align my heart's cry with His.

As I prayed that day, I felt God nudging me to write down our prayer points so that I would remember His desires for my children, who are His children. He wanted me to remember the experience that so confirmed for me His personal, knowing love for them. (You can read the prayer in Appendix 5, if you wish.) The prayer would serve as a record, on days less steady than this one, of what He is actively working to accomplish in my children's lives. The written notes from that prayer time would be evidence of His prevailing presence and heaven-sent activity in my children's hearts and lives.

Looking back now at those notes, I am encouraged by the structure and the boldness that God added to my prayers that day: I see that I know His plans for them to live lives of joy in Him and bold faith for the sake of His name (Jeremiah 29:11). God also used His inspiration during that prayer time to lift my eyes beyond the immediate moments of our days: the many teaching and correcting moments I wade through with my children are an important part of God's growing them into the plans He has for them. My daily work feeds into His great, active, real, heavenly purposes.

I remind myself that God's inerrant Word says that the words that go out from His mouth will not return to Him empty, but rather will accomplish what He intends them to and will succeed in the purpose for which He spoke them (Isaiah 55:11). Now I imagine that most any time I spend in prayer for my children is a powerful avenue through which God impacts their daily lives. Generously, He opened my eyes to perceive that on that day.

God knows us intimately and responds to our faith with His power. I want to put my children into His loving hands again and again and again, not thinking my prayers are feeble, but fully anticipating the tremendous good that He is working through them for His purposes in and through my children's lives. Our words in prayer can become His own desires that we are speaking back to Him! I must be faithful in praying for my children! God is using our prayers in unspeakably meaningful ways.

With love,
Lauren

> *"The wind blows where it wishes, and you hear its sound, but you do not know where it comes from or where it goes. So it is with everyone who is born of the Spirit."*
>
> *John 3:8*

†

Lord,

Thank You that by Your gift of faith, I trust You and know that my love for my children comes from You. Amazingly, You take the imperfect offerings of my faith and my love and You use them in accomplishing Your plans!

Your Word says that You will give us the desires of our hearts as we delight ourselves in You (Psalm 37:4). As promised, You take what I offer to You in prayer and You cause Your desires to become my desires, and passionately so! You fan my prayers into flame according to Your design. How full and overflowing with personal love and care You are for me and for the next generation, too!

Thank You that You meet me in prayer for my children, using that special avenue to participate with me in my parenting. Would you give me more of Your Holy Spirit as I pray, so that I am consistently praying according to Your desires? Thank You that as You hear my prayers and see my faith in You, You bless me with immeasurably more of Yourself. I am in awe that as I turn to You, You not only speak Your life into the challenges and needs that I place before You, but You also satisfy me with increasingly more of Yourself.

Amen.

Responding:

Day 1

List your children's names below and complete the chart to answer the following questions: What is your greatest desire for each of your children? What do you perceive as each of their greatest needs? Use your notes as a springboard to pray for them specifically.

Name	My greatest desire	Their need

Read Mark 5:21-24 and 35-42 and see how Jesus meets a parent in need. Write down Jesus' words from verse 36. Jesus operated in that parent's faith to bring physical life into his daughter's body. What spiritual life do you need to trust and believe Jesus is already working to bring about in your children's lives?

_____
_____
_____
_____

Use an online Bible search tool or the concordance in the back of your Bible to find a verse that relates to each of your children individually. If your child tends toward giving up easily, you could search for a verse about hope, like Romans 15:13, for example. Write down the verses you find and ask God to fan them into flame in your children's lives. Is there a regular day of the week that you could commit to consistently bringing these verses to God in prayer for your children?

Name	Verse

Pray: Read over what you have written down in response to today's questions. Close your eyes now and talk honestly with God about what you have written and about what you are thinking and feeling.

Day 2
God intends for the greatest desire of our hearts to be Him. Read Isaiah 33:5-6 and write verse 6. What does it mean to you to "fear the Lord"? How could "fearing the Lord" be your treasure?

_____
_____
_____
_____

Read John 16:12-15. In this passage, Jesus is teaching the disciples about the work of the Holy Spirit and it is a beautiful description of the joint activity of the Father, the Son, and the Holy Spirit in our lives. Write verse 15. How does it make you feel that the Holy Spirit, Jesus, and God the Father are declaring their truth into your life? How will you respond to God speaking His truth into your life?

_____
_____
_____
_____

Read 1 John 5:14-15 and write both verses here. Are you unsure about how to pray for each of your children? Ask God and see what He brings to mind.

_____
_____
_____
_____

Pray: Read over what you have written down in response to today's questions. Close your eyes now and talk honestly with God about what you have written and about what you are thinking and feeling.

> "For I will pour water on the thirsty land,
> and streams on the dry ground;
> I will pour my Spirit upon your offspring,
> and my blessing on your descendants."
> Isaiah 44:3

~28~
Rescue

October 15, 2019

Dear friend,

My husband, Jeff, was out of the house early every morning before work last week because of an extra work obligation, and then Saturday morning, and Sunday afternoon, and then this past Tuesday night. He is rarely that busy. I genuinely supported the reasons for his extra time away, but in the end it kept me from getting a decent break. The noise of three kids and the persistent demands of daily life with them were wearing on me. I felt drained and really needed refreshment. Can you relate?

While on most days God's guidance comes to me in quiet ways - a verse, a friend's encouragement, a friend's prayer - on the toughest days, I ask God to speak decisively and clearly. I sense my inability, and I crave the direction and protection His wings offer in life's storms (Psalm 91:4; Psalm 36:7).

I cried out to God quietly, in the silence of my mind during prayer time while my kids napped one afternoon. I felt very weary. I had been mothering alone and I wasn't at my best. I had been snapping at my kids and I had been short-tempered with them. I had lost my patience and couldn't regain it. As much as God had taught me, I was still finding myself doing things "my" way, operating in my own insufficient strength, instead of doing things the way He has taught me to. Disappointed to see myself doing that, I wondered when I would learn to actually do things His way. I knew what He had taught me to do, but I was struggling to consistently do it.

I came to God in faith and in surrender, but otherwise I was empty-handed. Do you know what? God arrived with a full-force spiritual rescue! He swooped in! All of a sudden during prayer, He restored me. God erased the weariness of my soul. I had felt completely sapped, and then suddenly, I was fully restored and refreshed. He took my burden away. I was completely free of it! After days of inward upheaval, suddenly I was a comforted soul basking in His peace. In the 23rd Psalm, King David expresses the same sentiment. He marveled at God's rescue of him: "He makes me lie down in green pastures. He leads me beside still waters. He restores my soul. He leads me in paths of righteousness for his name's sake" (verses 2-3). Sudden peace is a gift from the Lord and He is still granting it today.

If I were someone who had never experienced that kind of sudden freedom from a burden on my spirit, I think I would think that there must be more to it than the sudden healing I've described. But there wasn't! God acted powerfully and decisively in love towards me when I needed it, even though I did not deserve it. He is unconditionally faithful in loving us. Truly "the light shines in the darkness, and the darkness has not overcome it" (John 1:5).

God not only removed the burden I was feeling that day, but He spoke His life into my weary soul. He reminded me of a verse I had read from the book of Micah. He used it to teach me that this act of healing towards me reflected His consistently extravagant love towards us. God is always speaking into our lives like this, with the booming, victorious roar of a lion. I relate to the prophet Micah who was filled with joyful awe and cried out:

"Who is a God like you, pardoning iniquity and passing over transgression for the remnant of his inheritance? He does not retain his anger forever, because he delights in steadfast love. He will again have compassion on us; he will tread our iniquities underfoot. You will cast all our sins into the depths of the sea. You will show faithfulness to Jacob and steadfast love to Abraham, as you have sworn to our fathers from the days of old." Micah 7:18-20

In restoring my strength, God was singing victory over me! He was telling me about the victory that I have in Him simply by believing and trusting Him to be my source of spiritual life, now and forever. In response to my simple, obedient faith, God extended His ultimate faithfulness and allowed me to perceive new depths of His great love for me.

But, I wondered, what did the prophet Micah mean when He said that God will "show faithfulness to Jacob and steadfast love to Abraham" (Micah 7:20)? God connected the dots for me, reminding me of another passage I had read recently in the book of Isaiah, in which God's people are resolutely claiming their identity in Him by calling themselves "Jacob" and "Israel":

**"This one will say, 'I am the Lord's,
Another will call on the name of Jacob,
And another will write on his hand, 'The Lord's,'
And name himself by the name of Israel."
Isaiah 44:5**

We are the "Jacob" that Micah refers to! We are "Abraham" (Micah 7:20). It is to us that God will show faithfulness and steadfast love (Micah 7:20)! God had me see that even in a span of hard days, when I am overcome by my circumstances and by how I've handled them, I am resolutely and firmly His. In the face of my weakness, God remains utterly faithful towards me.

It matters that God is faithful towards me because, human as I am, my own weakness has not gone away yet, and it won't! All my life long, I will need to keep on leaning hard on Him. I need His faithfulness. He Himself knows I find myself faint and without might (Isaiah 40:29); He knows I will repeatedly fall exhausted (Isaiah 40:30). But as I lean on Him, He will continue to restore me (Isaiah 40:31). It is His promise to us, and He does it!

"He gives power to the faint, and to him who has no might he increases strength. Even youths shall faint and be weary, and young men shall fall exhausted; but they who wait for the Lord shall renew their strength; they shall mount up with wings like eagles; they shall run and not be weary; they shall walk and not faint." Isaiah 40:29-31

Not only does He renew my strength again and again, but as He promises, I do go on again, I run alongside Him, and I soar with strength (Isaiah 40:31). What a contrast to life lived in only my own inconsistent abilities. I find that God does do what He says He will do.

It is never me who restores my strength. It is never me who suddenly returns myself to joyful, strong, pure-hearted mothering. In my recurring weakness, I know that it is only God's victorious, lion-like faithfulness that refreshes me. He is the remedy, and I mother differently because of it. When I am feeling worn down to the frayed ends of my nerves and all that's left are my good intentions, I can await that moment that is sure to come: His repeated rescue of me! We repeatedly become depleted, to be repeatedly filled.

With love,
Lauren

> "For God alone, O my soul, wait in silence,
> for my hope is from Him.
> He only is my rock and my salvation, my fortress;
> I shall not be shaken."
> Psalm 62:5-6

✝

Lord,

I praise You that You hear the cry of my heart and not only the words of my mouth and the wandering of my ways. You restore me again and again, with a breath of Yourself to my soul. You restore me into the comfort of Your loving care and to the full, satisfying peace that comes only from You. You love to love me, even when I keep on straying from You and from what You have told me to do.

My imperfect nature inextricably intertwines me to You. I need You on an ongoing basis, and You provide. You provided once and for all through Jesus (John 3:16), but You do not stop there. You draw me continually into Yourself in a recurring cycle of refreshment. Again and again and again and again You rescue Your people and You will never be moved.

Amen.

Responding:

Day 1

Read Micah 7:18-20 and write verse 20. Into what weariness or concern of yours do you need God to speak His victorious life, faithfulness, and steadfast love?

_____

_____

_____

_____

Read Psalm 62:5-7. In verse 5, the psalmist says "my hope" is from Him. Fill in the blanks below (from the ESV translation of these verses) to write out verse 5. Notice what else the psalmist finds only in God.

> "For God alone, O my soul, wait in silence, for my <u>hope</u> is from him.
> He only is my _____ and my _____, my _____; I shall not be shaken.
> On God rests my _____ and my _____;
> My mighty _____, my _____ is God."
> Psalm 62:5-7

Which one of these words is especially meaningful to you today, and why?

Read Isaiah 40:27-28 and write verse 28. How do these verses encourage you to wait for God to act in a challenge you are presently facing?

Pray: Read over what you have written down in response to today's questions. Close your eyes now and talk honestly with God about what you have written and about what you are thinking and feeling.

Day 2
Read Isaiah 40:29-31 and make two lists below. In one column, write all of the words in these verses that you relate to feeling during a troubling time. In the other column, write all of the words from these verses that illustrate how God promises to rescue us.

There are times that I feel:	God promises:

Read Isaiah 41:8-10. From verses 9 and 10, write down all of the ways God promises that He carries His people. Notice from the verb tenses in this passage that His rescue of us covers the past, the present, and the future.

Read 1 Peter 5:6-11 and write verse 10. From this verse, who is it that restores us?

_____
_____
_____
_____

Pray: Read over what you have written down in response to today's questions. Close your eyes now and talk honestly with God about what you have written and about what you are thinking and feeling.

> "You are my servant, I have chosen you and not cast you off;
> I am with you; I am your God;
> I will strengthen you; I will help you;
> I will uphold you with my righteous right hand."
> Isaiah 41:10

~29~
He Loves Me

November 22, 2019

Dear friend,

Over the past few weeks I felt my heart hardening towards my oldest child. His persistently loud, abrupt, unrelentingly boyish behaviors had been pushing me to the far limit of my patience, and, coupled with his recent, regular tendency to whine in response to my direction, I felt my heart toward him feeling harder than I wanted it to. My intention was to have a pure heart as I held him to good, godly standards. But ragged from persevering, I felt myself hardening over time. I want to stand firmly, expecting God to work in him. Instead of waiting on God, I had started to respond out of bitterness and it was stealing my joy. Conflict seemed to be the focal point of so many days. I cried my eyes out one night in bed, disappointed and disillusioned.

I asked God to speak clearly to me in this area of need: How was I to go forward, feeling so upset, despite being right to hold him to a high standard? How was I to stay so committed but do it lovingly? It felt unattainable to me.

God answered me over the coming days, and He seemed to be telling me that I had asked the wrong question. In His awesome understanding, He had known the question I truly needed answered, and He answered that one instead. In my wiser moments as a parent, I can really relate to that - hearing the question asked of me and replying with my bigger-picture, more comprehensive, wiser understanding of the real need lying beneath. Isn't God wonderful to have such compassion and then to act on it towards us? He knew that answering my bigger question would satisfy the deeper need of my own heart, out of which I could in turn love my son well (Proverbs 4:23).

The deeper question God brought to the surface of my mind was one that had been nagging at my heart for several months: Does God love and accept me only when I am obeying Him? And relatedly: Am I earning or losing His approval and my place as His, moment by moment? When I fall short, am I disappointing Him?

God answered me through my naptime Bible reading and prayer time, my Bible study class homework, sermons, and books. He used it all. Here is what He said:

"I will give you a new heart, and a new spirit I will put within you. And I will remove the heart of stone from your flesh and give you a heart of flesh. And I will put my Spirit within you, and cause you to walk in my statutes and be careful to obey my rules" (Ezekiel 36:26-27). With these verses, God acknowledged my weakness; He told me that He sees my heart of stone and He has made a way for me to Him despite it. His response to my imperfection is Himself, the gift of His Holy Spirit alive in me. He knows I cannot always obey and He loves me - in action - anyway. One day, He will enable me to follow Him completely and I can count on it.

"The blood of Jesus his Son cleanses us from all sin" (1 John 1:7b). God impressed upon me that He sees me, and all of us who believe and trust in Him, through Jesus. Sin is not completely extricable from who I am, and God's plan accounts for that. He brought heaven to earth to satisfy the price for my inability to follow Him wholly (Isaiah 59:16). He is not surprised. I am not disappointing Him.

"Your guilt is taken away, and your sin atoned for" (Isaiah 6:7). As I did some daily reading in the book of Isaiah, I was surprised at how intensely I related to Isaiah when he said: "Woe is me! For I am lost; for I am a man of unclean lips... for my eyes have seen the King, the Lord of hosts!" (Isaiah 6:5). Like Isaiah did, I felt so undeserving and unholy in contrast to God's holiness. I am sure that it was God who caused me to feel the weight of that sentiment, and then He comforted me deeply as He replied that "[my] guilt is taken away, and [my] sin atoned for" (Isaiah 6:7). My holy reconciliation with the Father is already provided for through the death and resurrection of Jesus and my faith in Him (John 19:30; Revelation 12:11).

"The Lord Your God who goes before you will himself fight for you" (Deuteronomy 1:30). God went before me during this time, sending my mom to me in Virginia for a spontaneous two-day visit when He knew that I would become suddenly ill and need to stay in bed for a half-day. My mom cared for my children while I was unable to. In His extravagant love, God foresaw my need and sent my mom to care for me and for my children in my place. He went before me and fought for me. I received that gift as evidence of His love for me in action.

"But while he was still a long way off, his father saw him and felt compassion, and ran and embraced him and kissed him" (Luke 15:20). God showed me that, like the father and his wayward son in Luke chapter 15, my heavenly Father loves me and acts out of abundant grace towards me. He abounds with undeserved lovingkindness. His grace is bigger than my wrong attitudes and wrong words. He is the Father who answers me, even running toward me when I am still "a long way off". Also, God's love for me is not in conflict with His desire for me to live as He has told me to. It is in fact out of His love for me and His full hopes for me that He teaches me. He never holds me in contempt; He welcomes me in! He loves me.

God used all of these verses and experiences to eliminate my fear that His love for me wavers. I no longer wonder whether I am earning or losing His approval: I have it; I am His child. His Word promises it and my experience confirms it (Isaiah 55:11).

God caused me to see that my own knowledge of His love for me was a prerequisite to my being able to love my son unconditionally. And God has called me to love when it has not been earned; He has called me to love with His extravagant, undeserved love (John 13:34-35; Colossians 3:12-14). God is calling me to live out of the grace with which He so generously floods me. His grace is singularly sufficient for love in moments of my weakness and my children's weaknesses (2 Corinthians 12:9). I have to be secure in His love in order to love like He does.

The bitterness that had begun to take root in my heart has been melted by a growing acceptance of God's genuine love for me. God loves me freely; I am free to love like that. I am not disappointing God; I need not be disappointed by my children. God is growing me more and more into His image; I have the privilege of playing a part in God's forming my own children into His image. God is softening my heart toward my own children by convincing me of His love for me.

My heart no longer requires my children's obedience in order to be satisfied. No, God has satisfied the craving of my heart with His love. I teach my children so that they too will know His love and find real joy in Him. Out of hearts submitted to Jesus, living water truly flows (John 7:37).

Freed from my perceived need to earn His favor, assured that I have been bought with a price, I am free to rest in God's satisfying love and to overflow with it to my children. By His power, having "received without paying; [I can] give without pay" (Matthew 10:8).

With love,
Lauren

> "The friendship of the Lord is for those who fear Him, and he makes known to them his covenant."
> Psalm 25:14

†

Lord,

I have come to receive the grace that You have offered me. You have taught me to see with the eyes of my heart that You genuinely love me. I feel full - full of Your approval and of Your satisfaction in me as Yours. I feel I am firmly set in the current of Your love, and I feel free!

You have shown me that by Your power I can let Your abundant love flow out of me and into the lives of my family and everyone I meet. Ground me continually, Lord, please, in Your love, that I may live closely with You and draw others close to You through Your love alive in me. You are my alpha and my omega, my means and my end, the author and perfecter of my faith, and I love you.

Amen.

Responding:

Day 1

Read Ezekiel 36:26-27 and write verse 26. What effect does it have on you to know that God has a plan for giving us a new heart?

_____

_____

_____

_____

Read Ephesians 3:14-19 and write verse 19. What connection do you see or experience between Christ's love for you and your ability to love the people around you?

_____

_____

_____

_____

Read 1 John 4:9-11 and write verse 9. What life do you experience in Jesus that makes God's love real to you?

_____

_____

_____

Pray: Read over what you have written down in response to today's questions. Close your eyes now and talk honestly with God about what you have written and about what you are thinking and feeling.

Day 2

Read and write Psalm 90:14. From this verse, what effect does it have on us to be satisfied by, or to realize, the love God has for us?

_____
_____
_____
_____

Read Psalm 63:1-8. Write verse 7. What does it mean to you to mother "in the shadow of [God's] wings"?

_____
_____
_____
_____

Read 2 Corinthians 12:9-10. What particular weakness will you hand over to God today "so that the power of Christ may rest upon [you]"? How will the way you speak and act be different today because you are waiting for God to show up in that area?

_____
_____
_____
_____

Pray: Read over what you have written down in response to today's questions. Close your eyes now and talk honestly with God about what you have written and about what you are thinking and feeling.

"... that you, being rooted and grounded in love, may have strength to comprehend with all the saints what is the breadth and length and height and depth, and to know the love of Christ that surpasses knowledge, that you may be filled with all the fullness of God."

Ephesians 3:17-19

Closing Reflection

Take time to reflect back on what you and God have talked through together over the course of entries 21 through 29. Look back through your notes to answer these questions:

❀ What recurring topics and themes do you see showing up in your answers to the "responding" questions?

_____
_____
_____
_____

❀ Do you sense there is a resounding message that God wants you to hear from Him?

_____
_____
_____
_____

❀ How do you think God wants you to apply what He is telling you?

_____
_____
_____
_____

❀ Is there a particular verse that God has brought to your mind again and again over the course of your study? Write it here.

_____
_____
_____

❀ Use the verse you wrote down in response to the previous question to write an honest and heartfelt prayer to God in response to His closeness with you:

_____
_____
_____
_____

❀

Appendices

Appendix 1
Our Schedule
(See Entry #14: He Will Establish Your Plans)

This schedule - and having it so visible on our kitchen pantry door - worked so well for me and my kids when they were 2, 4, and 6. The clock times would get rearranged at random, we never filled in the black squares with little drawings as I intended, and two sets of clock hands even fell off. No matter! Knowing what we were going to do throughout the days was what mattered most and this colorful guide got the job done.

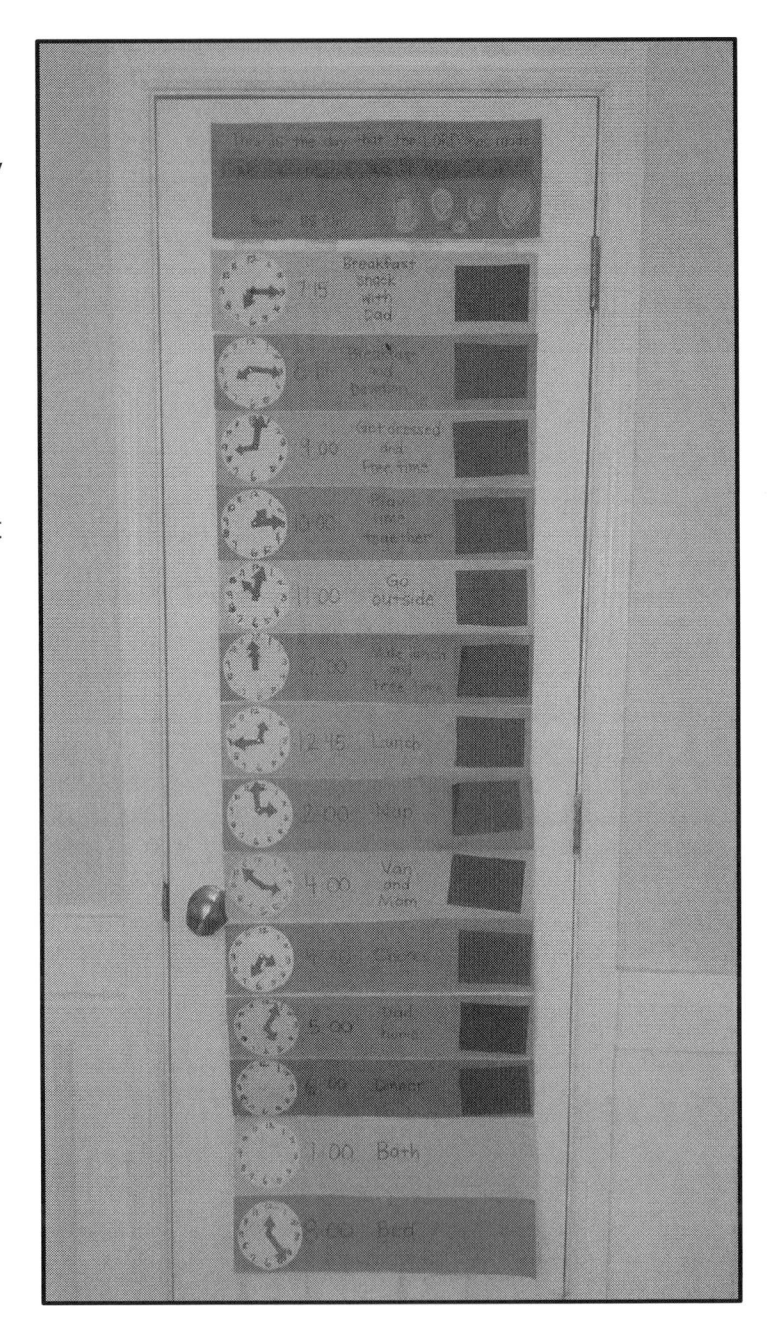

Appendix 2
Notes from My Journal
(See Entry #16: Our Cause)

Our Cause

My goal in raising my children
What do Jeff and I seek to do?
- Direct our children's attention to God so that they see the life we find only through living closely with Him.
- Train our kids to live God's way, so that they are people of character who enjoy Him, come alive in Him, and make Him more known and loved.

Strategies to align our parenting with that goal
At their young ages right now, how can we begin training them towards that goal?
- Keep God at the forefront of our own hearts.
- Keep God central to our family conversation and how we perceive everything in our lives - God is the lens.
- Train our kids in obedience and respect.
    - Ephesians 6:1 says "Children, obey your parents in the Lord, for this is right." We instruct them in God's ways and His ways are the best for us. We want our kids to:
        - Listen when we speak to them.
        - Obey the first time.
        - Cooperate agreeably, with a respectful attitude.
        - Grasp that even when they don't get what they want, God knows what is best for them and they can be content with what He has provided.

Our mindset
What do Jeff and I want the prevailing attitudes of our family to be as we work towards that goal?
- Joy and gratitude: It is important that we train our kids to choose joy and gratitude to God, as opposed to selfishness and self-pity when we do not get our way. Psalm 118:24. 1 Timothy 6:6 says "Godliness with contentment is great gain."
- Persistence: Training our kids to be persistent (and being persistent ourselves in training them and expecting results over time). Training them does not mean immediate first-time results. It means repeatedly "wearing that groove", as Jeff says. It means having consistent expectations again and again and again even when they fall short in that regard until a long way down the line.

- Love: We must teach them that God wants us to share His love with each other in action, by the way we treat each other. He said: "A new commandment I give to you, that you love one another: just as I have loved you, you also are to love one another" (John 13:34-35). Colossians 3:12-14 embodies love in action towards each other, too: "Put on then as God's chosen ones, holy and beloved, compassionate hearts, kindness, humility, meekness, and patience, bearing with one another, and if another has a complaint against another, forgiving each other; as the Lord has forgiven you, so you also must forgive each other. And above all these put on love, which binds everything together in perfect harmony."

The centrality of God's Word to our family's life
How will we weave God's Word into our daily life?
- What Bible verses will I train our children to memorize and apply to their daily lives?
    - "Jesus answered him, 'I am the way and the truth and the life. No one comes to the Father except through me.'" (John 14:6)
    - "So, whether you eat or drink, or whatever you do, do all to the glory of God." (1 Corinthians 10:31)
    - "Go into all the world and proclaim the gospel to the whole creation." (Mark 16:15)
- Prioritize making the time to do a Bible-based devotional each morning at breakfast with the kids.
- Be on the lookout to learn how to encourage them to spend their own time, as they get a bit older, with God in prayer and in His Word.

Appendix 3
Verses
(See Entry #16: Our Cause)

This is a photo of some of our Bible memory verse "flags" hanging up in our kitchen. I cut triangles out of colorful construction paper, punched holes in the tops of the triangles, and wrote our memory verses onto them. I made a note in pencil on the back of each triangle to remind myself which tune to use (see below chart). Once my two older children can sing a new verse by memory, I add that verse to the string of yarn, and then the next day we begin learning another.

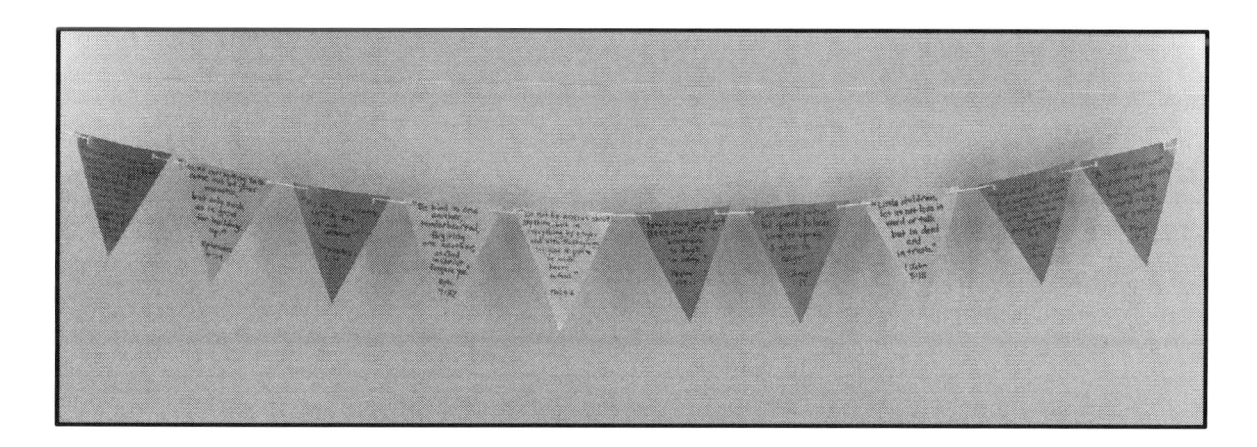

Below are some of the verses we have memorized and found readily applicable to everyday family life. We practice them during our breakfast devotion time.

Verse	Reference	Tune	How to Sing It
"Let no corrupting talk come out of your mouths, but only such as is good for building up."	Ephesians 4:29	"If You're Happy and You Know It"	Sing: *Let no corrupting talk come out of your mouths, Let no corrupting talk come out of your mouths, but only such as is good for building up. Ephesians 4:29*
"A soft answer turns away wrath, but a harsh word stirs up anger."	Proverbs 15:1	"She'll Be Coming Around the Mountain"	Sing: *A soft answer turns away wrath, But a harsh word stirs up anger. Proverbs 15:1 Proverbs 15:1 A soft answer turns away wrath.*

"Jesus said: 'This is my commandment: that you love one another as I have loved you."	John 15:12	"Oh When the Saints Come Marching In"	Sing: *Jesus said! This is my commandment! That you love one another as I have loved you! John 15:12. Love one another as I have loved you!*
"Only a fool despises a parent's discipline; whoever learns from correction is wise."	Proverbs 15:5	"The Noble Duke of York"	Sing: *Only a fool despises a parent's discipline. Whoever learns from correction is wise. Proverbs 15:5*
"Do all things without grumbling or disputing."	Philippians 2:14	Barney Theme Song ("I Love You, You Love Me")	Sing: *Do all things Without Grumbling or disputing. Philippians 2:14. Do all things without grumbling.*
"Fear not, for I am with you; be not dismayed for I am your God. I will strengthen you, I will help you, I will uphold you with my righteous right hand."	Isaiah 41:10	"Skip to My Lou"	Sing: *Fear not, For I am with you! Be not dismayed, For I am your God! I will strengthen you, I will help you, I will uphold you with my righteous right hand.*
"My son, if sinners entice you, do not consent."	Proverbs 1:10	"Mary Had a Little Lamb"	Sing: *My son, if sinners entice you, do not consent. Do not consent! My son, if sinners entice you, do not consent. Proverbs 1:10*
"You make known to me the path of life; in your	Psalm 16:11	"Joy to the World"	Sing:

presence there is fullness of joy."			*You make known to me the path of life! In your presence there is fullness of joy! Psalm 16, verse 11. The path of life. The path of life. You make known to me the path of life!*
"Jesus said: 'I am the way, the truth, and the life. No one comes to the Father except through me."	John 14:6	"If You're Happy and You Know It" (I used this tune again because it is easy to put verses to it!)	[Skip the words "Jesus said" and go straight to the words He said.] Sing: *I am the way, and the truth, and the life, I am the way, and the truth, and the life. No one comes to the Father except through me. In the Bible, John 14:6.*

Appendix 4
Balloon Moments
(See Entry #17: Think About These Things)

Draw a simple balloon shape on a piece of construction paper (I use a half-sheet of paper for each balloon), cut it out, and write your child's balloon moment on it - whatever he or she did that made God smile. Use your first balloon cut-out as a stencil and make a stack of blank balloons to have on hand for the next few days.

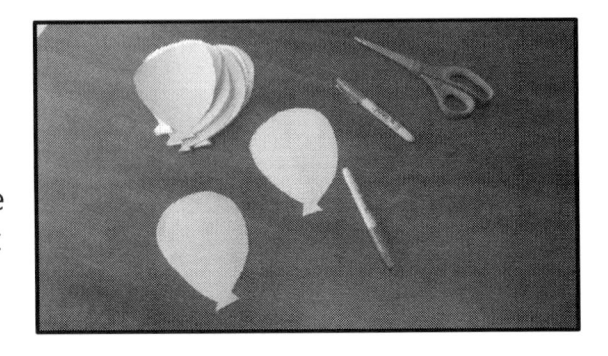

On some days I give my kids a balloon moment as a little surprise with their afternoon snack and it's waiting for them at the kitchen table after nap.

On other days I hang the balloons I make for my kids in our kitchen window so that we can keep admiring their special moments. I keep a roll of blue painter's tape in the kitchen so that I have it on hand for when I have balloon moments to hang up.

Appendix 5
Our Prayer
(See Entry #27: His Desires)

Our Prayer

Lord, Cause my children to embrace the truth of who You are. May they enjoy a personal, living relationship with You, their heavenly Father, from a young age.

May they know and see with all their hearts and with great clarity that You made them in specific, delightful ways. May Your voice resolutely remind them of who they are in You again and again throughout their lives. May Your voice be far louder and more influential than any earthly voice. May they know and see with their hearts that their comfort is not the goal of their lives. Rather, may they see wholeheartedly that they live in You and for You. May they see that they will be happiest following and enjoying You, wherever You lead them.

Remind them, please, of your straight and narrow path and bring them tremendous joy and satisfaction in living closely with You. "As He who called you is holy, you also be holy in all your conduct, since it is written, 'You shall be holy, for I am holy'" (1 Peter 1:15-16). I ask that You use their choices to reflect Your goodness and sovereignty to them and to those around them.

Cause them to be aware of Your callings on their individual lives. May they know that their giftings from You are to be used for Your glory. Cause them, full of faith, to actively say "yes" to being Your hands and feet in this world. Lead them to use their lives, their days, their words, their choices, and even challenging circumstances to "advance the gospel" (Philippians 1:12), even from a young age. Give them the satisfying joy of walking hand in hand with You in the good works You have already prepared for them to do. Make them Your powerful witnesses, out of their wholehearted trust that You are the only way. May they use Your blessings toward them to bless others.

Lord, I ask so often that You would equip me and Jeff in raising them, but I ask most especially that You work directly in them Yourself - accomplishing Your holy, transforming heart work that only You can do as You call them to You personally and undeniably. Please, Lord, keep them close to You, on Your path, for their joy and Your glory, according to Your design. We love to confidently and humbly call ourselves Yours.

Amen!

Small Group Reading Plan &
FACILITATOR'S GUIDE

Dear friend,

I am thrilled that you are considering using my book, <u>Good News for the Faithearted</u>, to lead a small group study with moms you know. Just like He used me to write the book, He will undoubtedly use your talents to facilitate these important conversations. God uses His people to guide others into His truth! And it is never about us – it is always about Him. That gives us confidence and peace as we carry out the assignments He has given us. You are ready, and He is able!

I designed the following pages to equip you in facilitating this study. I am praying for you as you step into the role of facilitator. God bless you!

With love,

Lauren

Overview:

This is designed as a 6-part study in which you will discuss five chapters of the book at each meeting. Moms should come to the first meeting having already completed chapters 1-5, and their written response questions, so that you can jump right in. They should complete the next 5 chapters and their questions in preparation for each subsequent meeting.

The ideal size for a small group is 5 - 10 moms. Larger groups can break down into smaller pods.

Suggested agenda for each meeting:

I suggest each meeting last about 1 hour and 15 minutes. Your familiarity with the moms in your group, and the size of your group, will influence how you organize your time, so feel free to adapt the following to your own group's dynamics. In short, you will lead the women to: PRAY – DISCUSS – PRAY. Here is a breakdown of your agenda:

Allow for informal gathering / chat time (10 mins)

Usually, this will be a few minutes of informal time to let everyone get settled and say hello. At the first meeting, though, introduce yourself and share the reason for your choice of this study. Then let the moms introduce themselves to the group, giving their name, their kids' names and ages, and the reason they want to participate in the study.

Open with a brief prayer (10 mins)

Start each meeting with prayer. Ask God to speak to the women in the group through your time together. If you want, you can use my prayer from pg. vii of the book. Or, you can adapt a Bible verse into a prayer, like Jeremiah 29:13-14: "You will seek me and find me, when you seek me with all your heart. I will be found by you, declares the Lord."

For meetings #2-6, consider looking back at the notes you made of last week's prayer requests (see below) and ask the women if they have any updates to share. That will also direct your opening prayer and give you a sense for where your moms are at the start of each meeting.

Facilitate the discussion (45 mins)

Each time your group meets, you will pose the same 6 questions to the group. I call these our "good news" questions. These are "good news" questions because when we see our weaknesses and our needs, and we bring them to Jesus, we find that God Almighty is present with us and ready to actively lead us!
Please turn to the last page of this facilitator's guide and you will find bookmarks that you can share with the women in your group. Printed on the bookmarks are the 6 "good news" questions you will pose to the group at each meeting. Each question begins with an anchor word in bold type. If each woman has a bookmark of her own, the anchor words will help her stay on track with the discussion no matter what her young children are doing in that moment!

You have 45 minutes set aside for discussion, so plan to spend about 7 minutes discussing each question. As the facilitator, be intentional about setting the tone for an honest and genuine conversation. You can do this by answering one of the first questions yourself. Share openly and vulnerably. The women will see that the intention of the group is to get real together and to learn together how to apply the truth of God's Word to everyday life.

Ideally, each mom will participate on each question in one way or another. Be comfortable with "pregnant pauses" to allow room for quieter moms to reflect and respond. Encourage active conversation with lots of give and take. If the women have a lot to discuss on one question, consider letting that natural conversation take place and simply adjust the time you can spend on a later question.

For your reference as facilitator, here are the 6 good news questions in a bit more detail than they are listed on the bookmarks:

1. **Needs:** Look back for a moment over what you wrote down over the course of today's chapters. What recurring needs do you see showing up in your responses? Where are you in need of God's help?

2. **Know:** What do you sense God nudging you to know about Him or your relationship with Him?

3. **Verse:** Is there a particular Bible verse that you want to make a point to remember? What is the significance of that verse for you?

4. **Input:** Based on your study, what input from the group are you seeking today?

5. **Apply:** How do you think God wants you to use what He is telling you in your everyday life?

6. **Pray:** How can the group pray for you?

Pray for one another (10 mins)
Make brief notes when the women answer question #6 above. Close the meeting by praying for the particular requests the women have mentioned. You can pray for all of the women yourself, or you can switch it up, asking other women if they are comfortable leading the prayer or having each mom pray for the woman on her right, for example. Model a straightforward prayer so that everyone will grow in their comfort level to pray in front of the group.

End the meeting with a reminder of which chapters you will cover at your next meeting and the date of that meeting.

Set up your calendar:
This 6-part study covers five chapters each time your group meets:
- Meeting #1: Cover chapters 1-5
- Meeting #2: Cover chapters 6-10 and reflection
- Meeting #3: Cover chapters 11-15
- Meeting #4: Cover chapters 16-20 and reflection
- Meeting #5: Cover chapters 21-25

❀ Meeting #6: Cover chapters 26-29 and reflection

Before each meeting, your moms will read the next five chapters of the book and complete the written response questions at the end of those chapters. Decide how you want to proceed through your study:

	Frequency of meetings	Independent study between meetings	Cadence	Duration
"Intensive" study	Weekly	5 chapters and associated response questions	1 day to complete each chapter (Ignore the "Day 1"/"Day 2" headings and instead answer all questions after each chapter at once.)	6 meetings over 6 weeks
"Steady" study	Every other week	5 chapters and associated response questions	2 days to complete each chapter	6 meetings over 12 weeks

Share the good news

I am confident that God will meet you and your group of moms as you seek to follow Him. He is most certainly pleased, present, and actively at work!

At the end of your study, would you please consider inviting the members of your small group to post a review of Good News for the Fainthearted to both Amazon and Goodreads? Your positive reviews will lead more moms to discover the book and how the good news Jesus offers pertains to motherhood.

Would you consider challenging a mom from your group to facilitate a new small group study herself? I am eager to see as many moms as possible hear from Jesus in the same undeniable way that He speaks to you and me in our weakest moments. Every mom needs Him! Would you encourage the moms in your group to be bold to invite other moms to come and see who He is? We can expect big results from God for our own generation and those yet to come!

I would love to hear how God is moving in your group of moms. Please reach me at lcdgoodnews@gmail.com to share the good news with me.

Bookmarks

Print this page of bookmarks and duplicate it so that every mom in your study will have one. Punch a hole through the circle at the top of each, and string a pretty ribbon through it to complete the bookmark. You can even laminate these so that they will last.

Good News Questions

Needs: What recurring needs do you see showing up in your responses? Where are you in need of God's help?

Know: What do you sense God nudging you to know about Him?

Verse: What verse will you make a point to remember?

Input: What input from the group are you seeking today?

Apply: How do you think God wants you to use what He is telling you in your everyday life?

Pray: How can the group pray for you?

Closing Remarks:

As I've begun over the last several years to read my Bible daily, thanks particularly to friends who have invited me to study the Bible with them, I find that God speaks to us through a miraculous blend of His written Word and the power of His Holy Spirit. He leads us along and causes our hearts to know the truth of His Word and to know Him personally. Maybe you have known the Lord for years already, or maybe you are experiencing closeness with Him for the first time. If you do not yet have a habit of spending time with God in prayer and reading the Bible each day, or if you arrive at the end of your workbook and want to continue in close communication with God but don't know how, I can't encourage you enthusiastically enough to get started on a plan to get into reading the Bible. It will be the most fulfilling part of your day and life. I read from the English Standard Version (ESV) Study Bible because its study notes provide so much helpful teaching and insight and it connects so many dots from one part of the Bible to others. You could begin by reading the book of the Gospel of John, the fourth book of the New Testament, if you need a starting place. Invite a friend or two to study with you and enjoy the pleasure of studying God's Word together and learning from one another's walk with God. I am praying for you as you take your next step in the joy of walking with Jesus.

Also, if you have enjoyed this study, would you please consider posting a review of Good News for the Fainthearted to both Amazon and Goodreads? Your positive review will lead more moms to discover the book and how the good news Jesus offers pertains to motherhood. Thank you!

> *"Now to Him who is able to do far more abundantly than all that we ask or think, according to the power at work within us, to him be glory in the church and in Christ Jesus throughout all generations, forever and ever. Amen."*
>
> *Ephesians 3:20-21*

Bibliography

Boswell, Matt and Matt Papa, *His Mercy Is More*. Getty Music Label, 2019, Accessed January 22, 2021. https://www.youtube.com/watch?v=JoeAKG3LVCU.

Housefires, *The Way*. Housefires, 2017, Accessed January 22, 2021. https://www.youtube.com/watch?v=uCfveSHHwXo.

Lloyd-Jones, Sally. *The Jesus Storybook Bible*. Grand Rapids, MI: Zondervan, 2007.

Piper, John. *"Boasting Only in the Cross"*. Sermon, Passion's OneDay, Memphis, TN, May 20, 2000.

Rosemond, John. "Yelling at Your Kid Fuels Their Bad Behavior." Omaha World-Herald. Accessed January 22, 2021. https://omaha.com/lifestyles/parenting/john-rosemond-yelling-at-your-kid-fuels-their-bad-behavior/article_e94070db-37dc-5d80-a77a-81d0a2465a99.html.

Sovereign Grace Music. 2015. *Spirit of God*. Comp. Dave Fournier and George Romanacce.

Sjogren, Bob. *Cat and Dog Theology*. Downers Grove, IL: InterVarsity Press, 2003.

Sjogren, Debby. *Parenting for God's Glory: Creatively Training Children in Honor and Respect*. Mechanicsville, VA: Mission Minded Publishers, 2018.

Tripp, Tedd. *Shepherding a Child's Heart*. Wapwallopen, PA: Shepherd Press, 1995.

Printed in Great Britain
by Amazon